WINDOW OF OPPORTUNITY

The Joint Working Group on Western Cooperation in the Soviet Transformation to Democracy and the Market Economy is a collaboration between two private institutions: the Center of Economic and Political Research, USSR, and the Strengthening Democratic Institutions Project of Harvard University's John F. Kennedy School of Government. Grigory Yavlinsky and Graham Allison are respective directors of these two institutions. The Strengthening Democratic Institutions Project is funded by the Carnegie Corporation and the Ann and Gordon Getty Foundation. The EPCenter receives funding from various enterprises in the Soviet Union and the budgets of several republics.

The Joint Working Group chaired by Graham Allison and Grigory Yavlinsky included Elisabeth Allison, Robert Blackwill, Stanley Fischer, Alexey Makushkin, Alexey Melnikov, Alexey Mikhailov, Jeffrey Sachs, Elizabeth Sherwood, William Ury, Tatiana Yarygina, and Mikhail Zardornov. Assistance was provided by Bruce Allyn, Jill Barshay, Ellen Flynn Bedrosian, Richard Cavanagh, William Hogan, Dean LeBaron, David Lipton, Gary Mueller, William Parent, Olga Radaeva, Janet Sebile, Steve Singer, Astrid Tuminez, Patricia Walsh, Malcolm Wiener, and Lee Wolosky. In addition, we have benefited from consultation with and advice from many others in the U.S. and the USSR.

Chapters 2 and 4 were initially drafted in Moscow by Soviet experts at EPCenter and subsequently refined in consultation with Western experts. Chapter 3 draws upon earlier work prepared by American members of the Working Group. All participants made significant contributions to the Joint Program and agreed upon its content.

WINDOW OF OPPORTUNITY

THE GRAND BARGAIN
FOR DEMOCRACY
IN THE SOVIET UNION

Graham Allison and Grigory Yavlinsky

CO-CHAIRMEN, JOINT WORKING GROUP

HARVARD UNIVERSITY
JOHN F. KENNEDY SCHOOL OF GOVERNMENT
STRENGTHENING DEMOCRATIC INSTITUTIONS
PROJECT
U.S.A.

CENTER FOR ECONOMIC AND POLITICAL
RESEARCH (EPCENTER)
USSR

PANTHEON BOOKS, NEW YORK

This report was originally subtitled:
JOINT PROGRAM
FOR WESTERN COOPERATION
IN THE SOVIET TRANSFORMATION
TO DEMOCRACY
AND THE MARKET ECONOMY

A CIP record has been established for this title with the Library of
Congress

ISBN: 0-679-74028-7

BOOK DESIGN BY CATHRYN S. AISON

Manufactured in the United States of America

FIRST EDITION

CONTENTS

PREFACE

This Joint Program for the Soviet Union's transformation to democracy and the market economy was prepared for the heads of government of the Soviet Union, the United States, and the other industrial democracies. It was presented first to President Bush and Secretary of State Baker in the United States, and to Presidents Gorbachev, Yeltsin (of Russia) and Nazarbayev (of Kazakhstan) in the Soviet Union, and thereafter to the heads of the G-7 governments. (Canada, United Kingdom, Germany, France, Italy, and Japan). It was delivered in June 1991, to assist in their preparation for the extraordinary meeting between President Gorbachev and the G-7 heads of state in London in July.

Our objective in preparing this report was to raise higher on these governments' agenda what we believe is the single most important international issue in 1991. That question is: What about the Soviet future? With the end of the cold war, how will the leaders of the Soviet Union and the republics choose to reconstruct their nation? What are the West's stakes in alternative Soviet futures and what can it do to advance these interests?

When the leaders of the G-7 governments met a year earlier, in July 1990, in Houston, the issue of the Soviet future had been discussed in less than an hour, dismissed in a paragraph of the final communiqué, and buried in a multi-agency study of the Soviet economy. As private citizens who are students of Soviet and American affairs, we judged that this conclusion was mistaken then. We believed that any equivalent conclusion would be even more misguided in 1991.

Moreover, on the Soviet side, by early 1991 it was evident that President Gorbachev's economic *perestroika* had failed. The Soviet economy was in sharp decline. We knew that President Gorbachev believed that leaders of the G-7 who live in successful market economies knew more about market economies than he or others in the Soviet Union. For us, this was the origin of the idea that if he were invited to meet with the leaders of the G-7 governments at their Summit, he would have to focus clearly on the question of Soviet economic reform. He would want to present to them a program that they would approve.

Our collaboration had begun in November 1990. As it happened, I was in Moscow meeting with Grigory Yavlinsky on November 20, the day his resignation as First Deputy Prime Minister of the Russian Federation took effect. As the Russian press quipped, his was the first successful resignation since Czar Nicholas II. Others had simply disappeared.

Yavlinsky's resignation was triggered by Gorbachev's September 1990 rejection of the 500-Day Plan, of which he and Stanislav Shatalin had been the co-authors. Under these circumstances the Russian Federation was unable to pursue an economic program with any prospects of success, so Yavlinsky concluded that he would not front for their fraud. He resigned, explaining publicly why he was resigning. As a professional economist, he forecasted what he judged would be the inevitable results of the economic program Gorbachev had adopted. Specifically, he predicted massive government deficits, falling output, rapidly rising prices, a balance of payments crisis, and the impending specter of economic collapse.

I concurred strongly with his diagnosis and worried deeply about what such an outcome could mean for American interests. Economic crisis and collapse was likely to trigger either the overthrow of Gorbachev by a counterrevolutionary iron hand or, alternatively, disintegration of the Soviet Union into civil wars and chaos. Either outcome would pose major threats to American vital interests. Thus, objectively, there was a powerful interaction between Soviet decisions and Western interests—an interaction that should motivate an enlightened Western policy to attempt to effect outcomes more consistent with Western interests. As Yavlinsky remarked at the time, he had learned that it was too hard for one person sitting in Moscow to play chess with himself.

We agreed there to work together to prepare a Joint Program to overtake the crisis. We assembled a Joint Working Group of outstanding Soviet and American academics, most of whom had relevant practical experience. The Report that emerged was presented in nontechnical language in the hope that it could be read by heads of government and their relevant ministers as well as by professional staffs.

Events conspired to give the report a grander reception than we had ever imagined. On April 23, 1991, President Gorbachev and the heads of the nine major republics of the Soviet Union reached the historic Nine-Plus-One agreement that satisfied all the political preconditions for real economic reform. By devolving substantial power to the republics, that treaty would create a government with the legitimacy and the capacity to carry through a real economic reform program.

As evidence of the failure of the Soviet economic program mounted, and the possibility that he might be invited to meet with the G-7 governments in London appeared, President Gorbachev expressed strong interest in the program we were preparing. At Gorbachev's initiative, Yavlinsky was selected as a member of a special team that Gorbachev sent to Washington for discussions with American officials prior to his coming to the G-7 Summit. There, Yavlinsky met with President Bush, Secretary Baker, and others who expressed great interest in the program we were preparing. One thing led to another and by the time the Program was delivered in mid-June, it was widely read at the highest levels of each of the governments. Separately and together, Yavlinsky and I spent many hours discussing the ideas in this report with Presidents Gorbachev and Yeltsin and top-level officials in all the G-7 governments. At these meetings we discussed not just the general concepts in the proposed Joint Program but the specific details.

For example, when we met with President Gorbachev on June 24, he was clearly struggling to define his own program to take to London. He had met the previous week with Jacques DeLors, President of the European Commission, who had explained to him that the only way in which he could hope to control inflation was through sharp reductions in the government's massive deficits. In our meeting, at one point he leaned across the table, stared at me quizzically, repeated what DeLors had told him, and asked: "Is this the only way?"

In the end, our effort failed—at least in the first round. President Gorbachev proved unwilling, or unable, to adopt a coherent economic reform program. Instead, he sent a letter to the leaders of the G-7 governments with his own program. One American official dubbed it "the Pavlinsky Plan"—more Pavlov than Yavlinsky. As a result, Yavlinsky decided not to go to London with the Gorbachev team for the meeting with the G-7 governments.

Given Gorbachev's submission, the G-7 governments found it rather easy to agree on a response. In essence, they said: Good first try but no cigar. As a consolation prize, they gave the Soviet Union "special association" status in the IMF and the World Bank, and recommended that the Soviet government work with experts from those institutions to prepare a coherent economic reform program, along the lines of the one outlined in our Joint Program.

In fact, in the preparation for the G-7 discussion of the Soviet Union and potential Western assistance to its reform, there had been sharp differences of opinion among the G-7 governments. The "continentals," led by Germany, backed strongly by Italy and eventually by France, were eager to do more sooner. The "islanders," being somewhat further away from the problems and their consequences, wanted to do less. In each case, the "islanders'" reticence was motivated principally by domestic issues external to their strategic stakes in Soviet reform.

Our answer to the fundamental question about the Soviet future is presented in the Report. Analyzing as best we could historical developments in the Soviet Union and the West, and pondering the words and actions of the leaders of the key governments, we identified three basic principles that could guide deep, mutual engagement in the Soviet transformation to democracy and a marker economy.

In government, the principle is *democratization*. In the realm of economics, the basic principle is the *creation of a market economy and integration into the world economy*. In the security dimension, the principle is *cooperation in shaping a new world order*. In sum, the strategic concept for the next phase of Soviet history should be a decisive commitment to *transform* the Soviet Union into a democracy and a market economy; to rejoin the international community and be *integrated into world society*. The strategic concept for the West should be one of *active engagement* in rehabilitating the Soviet Union from a deep and long illness. Western leaders should commit their nations to assist in every practical way to increase the likelihood of success of the Soviet Union's transformation to a normal, civilized society.

The simple idea with which we began, and ended, was the concept of *strategic interaction*. The path of economic transformation Soviet leaders can choose and reasonably hope to succeed in following depends critically on the extent of Western support. Simultaneously, the extent of Western support depends critically on the program of economic reform that the Soviet Union is prepared to choose and follow. Rather than each waiting for the other to act—or attempting to play chess by itself—we proposed that the governments work together to develop a Joint Program, beginning with actions the Soviet Union would take in its own interests but allowing it firmer expectations about what would be forthcoming from the West in its own interests. That proposition remains as valid today as when originally stated.

Several features of the process by which this document was produced contributed to significant public misunderstanding of our central ideas. Because we were preparing the Report in the first instance for the leaders of the governments, the document was private. Before we had completed the document, public debate about the ideas ignited. Most of those debating the ideas had, of course, not read the document. The metaphor of a "grand bargain" had been coined in a May 1991 *Foreign Affairs* article by Robert Blackwill and me. As stated there, the central concept of the "grand bargain" is a process of long-term strategic interaction and support by the West on a step-by-step and strictly conditional basis if, and only if, the Soviet Union and its participating republics take practical and tangible steps toward democracy and a market economy.

It may be worth reiterating what the program is not. It is not a *giveaway* of anything to anybody: of Western money to the Soviets or their soul to us. Rather, if for their own reasons, they choose decisively the road to democracy and the market economy, the Program calls for our engagement and support as an investment in our security. It is not billions of dollars upfront to the Soviet Union on the faint hope or vague promise of reform. Indeed, the Program calls for no money down. It is not a program to prop up a tottering, corrupt, Communist system. As the Report states, that system cannot be reformed. It must be replaced. This is a program for speeding its replacement by a market-oriented democracy that can be sustained. The Program is not pro-Gorbachev vs. Yeltsin or any other personality; or pro-center vs. the republics. It is *pro* the process of democratization and rapid movement to the market economy. And it is not unconditional. Western assistance is strictly contingent upon the Soviets taking the necessary actions for such assistance to be used effectively. These actions include real economic reform and continued democratization, respect for the rights of individuals in the participating republics, and cooperation on critical issues of foreign policy.

As this is written, the spectacular acceleration of the ongoing revolution toward democracy and the market economy brings the basic concepts in *Window of Opportunity* to the top of the agenda. In the wake of the defeat of the bureaucratic, authoritarian coup, Yavlinsky was chosen as one of the four-man committee to manage the government in the transition and to make recommendations about the new governing arrangements. He was specifically charged with proposing a new comprehensive economic reform program for movement to the market economy and integration into the world economy. That program will bear more than a little resemblance to the economic program for the Soviet Union outlined here.

The good news of the defeated coup was the dismissal or discrediting of the principal obstacles to real economic reform in the Soviet Union. These were the five whales: Pavlov's central ministry bureaucracies, the Communist Party *apparatchiks,* the military, the KGB, and Interior Ministry *securitat.* The bad news is that the good guys have now inherited all the problems of a failing Soviet economy plus one: the release of powerful national impulses for independence. The challenge of creating a new confederation or community of independent republics, sufficient to sustain a common economic space in which the parties can move rapidly to a market economy, is daunting and may prove overwhelming. Nonetheless, the Program for rapid movement to the market economy outlined here is, we believe, the Program any individual republic, and any combination of republics will have to follow if it is to have reasonable prospects of success.

Moreover, the basic principles for Western engagement in this process outlined in the Joint Program still apply. By announcing what it will do *if and when* the governments of the republics take the necessary action for assistance to be used effectively, the West can use its influence to improve the odds that Soviet democracy and market economies will succeed. Those necessary conditions include not only initial steps in a coherent economic reform program but also respect for individual rights in the republics, and economic and political cooperation among republics, in order to be eligible for such assistance.

In the first week of September, it remains unclear what political configuration will emerge in the former USSR and how decisively it will act. It remains unclear whether and to what extent the West will engage and be forthcoming. Certainly there remains a gap between what we proposed and what has already been done by either party.

Nonetheless, we take heart from Winston Churchill's observation that democracy is the form of government that eventually gets to the right conclusion—after having exhausted all conceivable alternatives.

Graham Allison
September 9, 1991

WINDOW OF OPPORTUNITY

1

THE BASIC ARGUMENT:
CONCEPTS AND VALUES

There is a tide in the affairs of men,
Which, taken at the flood, leads on to fortune;
Omitted, all the voyage of their life
Is bound in shallows and in miseries.

—Shakespeare,
Julius Caesar

OVERVIEW

This report begins with the concept of *strategic interaction.*
The leaders of the Soviet Union and republics will make
hard decisions about their reforms based on their analysis of their best interests. But the road to reform they can
realistically follow depends critically on the nature and
degree of Western engagement. Conversely, while Western leaders will decide about their engagement with the
Soviet Union on the basis of their calculation of Western
interests, the extent of cooperation is critically dependent on the path of reform the Soviet Union is prepared
to undertake.

If these propositions are correct, one implication becomes inescapable. Rather than each party hesitating

and waiting for the other to act, the governments of the Soviet Union and the West must urgently ask and answer: *what if?* Together, these governments should jointly develop a common program of step-by-step initiatives each would undertake *if* the other were prepared to act. Our purpose is to suggest an outline of such a joint program.

The concept of strategic interaction is not new. It lay at the heart of the Marshall Plan. Some forty-four years ago last June, U.S. Secretary of State George C. Marshall delivered the commencement address at Harvard in which he issued a challenge to the countries of Europe. If these nations could jointly develop a plan "to place Europe on its feet economically," the United States would support and finance such a plan "so far as it may be practical for us to do so."

Though this fact is lost to the footnotes of history, the nations invited to participate in the Marshall Plan included the Soviet Union and the countries of Eastern Europe. Stalin declined.

Marshall's proposal was greeted with skepticism at home. Some argued that after five years of wartime neglect, America's domestic problems demanded first claim on the nation's limited resources. Others found bizarre the thought that scarce American dollars would go to countries that included former enemies who had so recently fought America's sons in war. Perhaps most incredible to "experts" was the presumption that after four centuries of almost continuous inter-European wars, these nations could become a community at peace.

Nonetheless, Marshall persisted in the conviction that American interests required deep engagement with European nations as they built their futures. Intense cooperation among themselves, stimulated by generous assistance from America, would make possible a peace and prosperity of which prior generations could scarcely dream. The realization of that dream shaped our world.

The Political Challenge

The revolutionary times in which we live place a special conceptual burden on the leaders of today's great nations. The forces of history confront both Soviet and Western leaders with new and fundamental questions: questions deeper and more troubling than mortals can comfortably answer. In the aftermath of the Cold War:

- What kind of country will the Soviet Union become? What role will this Soviet Union play in international affairs?

- What interests does the West have in the Soviet answer to questions about Soviet society? Should the West's goal be to promote the disintegration of the Soviet Union or, rather, to assist its transformation into an advanced industrial democracy consisting of voluntarily associated republics? Specifically, how should the West relate to ongoing changes there?

- What concept of a stable relationship between the Soviet Union and the West will meet each side's hardheaded analysis of its national interests and the requirements for international order?

Six years of *perestroika* have profoundly changed Soviet society and aspirations. Many of these changes are irreversible. *Glasnost* has opened eyes and minds that will not be closed again. Steps toward political democratization have energized Soviet society, as shown by the vigor of the republics and their demands to shape their own futures. Witness also the rapid growth in political awareness of ethnic groups and the increasing influence of the labor movement on policy making. On June 12, for the first time in its history, Russia chose a democratically elected president.

Changes in politics stimulate changes in economics. Relaxation of the fear that has been the dominant chord of Soviet society has undermined the command system of economic management. A genuine entrepreneurial sector is emerging. And while recent economic deterioration has meant severe hardship for many, especially pensioners and children, the need to provide for one's own family has changed people's thinking from reliance on the state to self-reliance. The process of *glasnost* has brought to light these developments and has revealed fundamental problems long suppressed and obscured by the old system. Their combined impact has shattered the system.

Spurred by these developments, the leaders of the Union and of nine republics made a political breakthrough on April 23. Their (Nine-Plus-One) Agreement sets up genuine power-sharing arrangements among sovereign republics. The leaders are now actively negotiating a new voluntary Union Treaty, which will be followed by a new constitution and new free elections for national offices. All that remains is for this ambitious political program to be carried out.

The Economic Crisis

What now demands immediate attention is the Soviet economic crisis. The Soviet Union finds itself in a complex predicament where retreat is impossible, but the road ahead frightens a nation whose people have lived in a totally different world.

The attempt to cope with this crisis has brought the leaders of the Soviet Union and the republics to the point at which history's "tide is at the flood". If the Soviet Union continues down the present path of half-hearted economic reform, today's decline will become tomorrow's free-fall. Economic collapse will not only defeat the promised political reforms, but is likely to lead to the disintegration of the Soviet Union, perhaps in a violent manner. Alternatively, President Gorbachev, President Yeltsin, President Nazarbayev and the leaders of the other republics now have a chance to choose a radically different path to a market economy and integration into the world economy.

Their choice is not one the West can view with indifference, as if from a distant planet: not only because this nation covers one-sixth of the earth's land mass, has 300 million people, vast natural and intellectual resources, and a huge military arsenal that includes one-half of the world's nuclear weapons, and not only because the protracted ideological confrontation with the country shaped the history of the twentieth century—but because the USSR shares with the West a common physical and political space. Changes happening now in the USSR have consequences for the whole world.

The Soviet Union is and will remain a great power. Like any other nation it will adhere only to those policies it judges to be in its own best interest. If Soviet leaders are now willing to attempt a decisive breakthrough to democracy and the market economy, Western leaders will confront their own fateful choice. To engage or not to engage—that will be the question. And if to engage, whether to stretch to a level of engagement that maximizes the likelihood of success. For the clear lesson of recent history is that without deep Western cooperation and assistance, the Soviet Union's chances of reaching its destination successfully in the foreseeable future will be low.

COMMON VALUES AND INTERESTS

The aspiration of the people of the Soviet Union today is for their nation to become a "normal society," a "civilized society." No objective observer can fail to be greatly impressed by the courage of Mikhail Gorbachev, Boris Yeltsin, and other Soviet leaders in facing harsh realities. President Gorbachev's Nobel Peace Prize speech expresses the heart of the matter:

> We want to become an integral part of modern civilization, to live in harmony with mankind's universal values, abide by the norms of international law, follow the "rules of the game" in our economic relations with the outside world.

Freedom is the bottom line. Freedom means the right of each human being to exercise his unconstrained rights concerning fundamental issues including speech, press, religion, and assembly.

In the realm of government, freedom means *democracy*.

A legacy from ancient Greece, the concept of democracy has been refined in practice through the centuries. Constitutional guarantees of individual rights by a government that derives its power from the consent of the governed are protected by contested elections in which citizens select their leaders. The leaders and citizens of the Soviet Union are taking historically unprecedented steps toward democracy, week by week.

In economics, the core value of freedom is exercised in a *market economy* based on private ownership in which market forces of supply and demand answer the question of who produces what for whom. Ownership means the freedom to use or dispose of property as an individual chooses. Basic laws of economics tolerate no equivocation on this point, none whatsoever.

In international relations, the core values are *peace and freedom:* an international order that permits nations to determine their own evolution free from force, the threat of force, and outside interference.

Can Soviet leaders embrace these values and act effectively upon them? The best evidence is the recent transformation of Soviet foreign policy. In relations with Eastern Europe, President Gorbachev repealed the "Brezhnev Doctrine" and allowed nations to choose their own way. Presidents Gorbachev and Kohl negotiated rapid unification of a sovereign Germany. The Soviet leadership set out on a radical venture to conclude the Cold War by eliminating massive conventional armaments in Europe through the negotiation of CFE. When faced by the choices posed by Saddam Hussein's invasion of Kuwait last August, Soviet Foreign Minister Shevardnadze joined U.S. Secretary of State Baker in condemning the action and cutting off arms to Iraq. In the weeks that followed, the Soviet Union voted for each U.N. resolution condemning Iraq and demanding its withdrawal, and played an important role in persuading others to join them.

While many events in the Soviet Union provide grounds for continued skepticism that a fundamental shift in values has taken place, the Soviet leadership's success in transforming Soviet participation in international affairs cannot be denied. We believe the central lesson is this: In the international arena, bold Soviet leadership on the one hand was *engaged* by bold Western leadership on the other. At Malta, in Washington, and in other capitals, each side moved carefully, step by step. The achievements are now a matter of historical record. They were based on conceptual transformations of the most fundamental kind. They demonstrated a vision, on both sides, unusual in the affairs of state. They changed our world.

WHAT IS NOW POSSIBLE?

Success in shaping a new international relationship between the West and the Soviet Union now presents new opportunities. But once more, a conceptual breakthrough is required. Analyzing as best we can historical developments in the Soviet Union and the West, and pondering the words and actions of the leaders of the key governments, we see emerging answers to history's questions. Specifically, we have identified three basic principles that could guide deep mutual engagement in the Soviet transformation to democracy and a market economy.

- In government, the principle is *democratization*. Specifically, this means: (1) a political structure based on power-sharing between the center and sovereign republics that devolves significant power to the republics, dissolves the unitary state, and establishes a new federal structure among those republics that choose to participate; (2) acceptance of the sovereignty of the republics including their right to exit; (3) freely contested, democratic elections for political leaders at all levels; (4) an end to the monopolization of political power by any one party; and (5) guarantees for individual human rights.

- In the realm of economics, the basic principle is the *creation of a market economy and integration into the world economy*. Specifically, this means: (1) legalization of basic economic rights, beginning with the ownership of property; (2) privatization of the vast majority of state enterprises; (3) demonopolization so that new enterprises can be created and all enterprises can compete; (4) budgetary and monetary stabilization through rapid cuts in subsidies and expenditures for defense and military-industrial enterprises; (5) liberalization of prices to allow them to be determined by market forces of supply and demand; and (6) normalization of international trade through the acceptance of established international trading practices including a convertible currency.

- In the security dimension, the principle is *cooperation in shaping a new world order*. The breakthrough has already been made. Its thrust must be extended. Operationally, this means: (1) rapid implementation of CFE and completion of START; (2) sharp, mutually agreed reductions in military forces and military expenditures; (3) cessation of aid for nations and forces promoting regional conflicts; (4) accelerated cooperation in international problem-solving including regional disputes and global threats, the proliferation of ballistic missiles, weapons of mass destruction, and terrorism.

In sum, the strategic concept for the next phase of Soviet history should be a decisive commitment to *transform* the Soviet Union into a democracy and a market economy; to rejoin the international community and be *integrated into world society.* The strategic concept for the West is one of *active engagement* in rehabilitating the Soviet Union from a deep and long illness. Western leaders should commit their nations to assist in every practical way to increase the likelihood of success of the Soviet Union's transformation to a normal, civilized society.

HOW WOULD THIS BE POSSIBLE?

How might such principles apply to the political and economic transformation of the Soviet Union? Three tests must be met. The first is the necessity for *mutual advantage.* No government will undertake the actions required out of charity or because outsiders demand they do so. Only hard national interests can sustain commitments to the hard actions required. Fortunately, mutual engagement in the Soviet's transformation to political and economic democracy meets this test. For the Soviet Union, it offers the only prospect for completing the reform process and beginning to close the gap between Soviet standards of living and those of economically advanced countries. For the West, success would not only lead to escape from a security nightmare—it would constitute the single greatest advance for peace in the postwar world.

The second test is that strategic interaction occurs *step by step*. This means a joint plan built from a coherent conceptual framework that begins with the essential pillars of a market economy. Each step by one must trigger a corresponding step by the other. The major stages and measures of Soviet economic reform must be synchronized with measures taken by the West to assist these reforms.

The third test is one of *conditionality*. No more than any other country can the Soviet Union be expected to tolerate unwarranted intervention in its internal affairs. At the same time, it is obvious that Western assistance will be strictly contingent upon a process Western governments judge to have reasonable prospects for success. These conditions will be monitored step by step throughout the process by both parties. As in any good partnership, some conditions will be more explicit, some understood. Over the past four decades, the international financial institutions have developed standard, mutually accepted procedures for providing conditional financial assistance, procedures that should apply to this case as well. Furthermore, since all parties are interested in political as well as economic transformation, the scale of Western assistance will inevitably be related, step by step, to progress in fulfilling the Soviet Union's own timetable for democratization established in the Nine-Plus-One Agreement.

If, for reasons of deepest Soviet national interest, the Soviet leadership chooses to "go for it"—to establish a market economy and democracy—this initiative must be welcomed by the West in more than words. It must be embraced by deeds.

Money is not the beginning of the matter, nor the end. Nor is it the most important element. We can imagine few more certain formulas for failure than for the West to put a bag of billions of dollars on the table and leave the rest to hope. Soviet leadership at all levels faces no more difficult task than to know *how* to take concrete steps that will transform its society. Lessons learned from centuries of trial and error in building democracies and functioning economic systems must be distilled, adapted, and adopted, not only in the Kremlin but throughout society. Moral, intellectual, and technical engagement are vital. As at the time of the Marshall Plan, today Soviet leaders and citizens need most of all the *confidence* that would come from the message Europeans heard: their best efforts would not fail for want of assistance that the U.S. could practically provide.

In the transformation to the market economy, Soviet resources, Soviet courage, and Soviet determination will be the single most important factor. The Soviet Union can and must mobilize the enormous potential that exists in a country so rich in human and natural resources. No outsider can do for the Soviet Union what it will not do for itself.

But let us also be clear. If the Soviet leadership decides to transform the Soviet Union into a market economy, the path it can reasonably hope to travel will be critically affected by the degree of Western cooperation, including the scale of financial assistance. The hurdles they can hope to clear, the pace at which they can move, the pain the Soviet people will have to suffer and—most

important for the West—the risks of potentially cata-
strophic failure depend on the West as well as the Soviet
Union.

How much financing will be required to support such
an agenda? Our analysis of financial needs yields no
magic number. In the final analysis, the financial needs
will emerge in the course of the design and execution of
the program. In this joint plan, we present our best professional judgment of the financing that would be required to support a coherent Soviet program for moving
as rapidly as is possible to a market economy. We indicate the kind of Western assistance that could make a
significant difference in the probability of success. Our
judgments about types of needed Western financial assistance are informed by the analysis presented in the
joint report on the Soviet economy produced by the
IMF, the World Bank, the OECD, and the EBRD for the
leaders of the G-7. We have also drawn upon our own
analysis of the growing intensity of economic collapse in
the Soviet Union, and our observations of Western support programs for other economies in distress, particularly the recent favorable experiences of Eastern
European countries.

In our view, a transformation program of the magnitude that we urge here would require substantial external assistance for several years. We expect that larger
amounts will be needed at the outset, and declining
amounts as private investment grows. These funds
would be required not for general assistance but for
specific purposes: balance of payments assistance during
price liberalization, a currency stabilization fund for the
transition to convertibility, and private enterprise funds
to foster the development of new, private businesses.

Shared among industrial democracies and international financial institutions, the annual budgetary costs to the governments of the largest economies would not be large.

Specific financing requirements will be the subject of intensive study and constant review once the reform process is underway. We urge Western governments to direct the international institutions—the IMF, the World Bank, the OECD, and the EBRD—to play a central role in refining the economic agenda and financing estimates, as the Western strategic engagement in the Soviet Union's democratic and economic transformation moves from words to deeds.

2

IS SOVIET
POLITICAL AND ECONOMIC
REFORM POSSIBLE?

The Soviet Union has come to a dramatic moment in which it must confront major challenges simultaneously and immediately. As old social institutions are rejected, new values are gaining acceptance. The country's future cannot be determined from the outside but will be shaped by society's understanding of the necessity for its transformation. This objective process has now become irreversible. But what will the price be?

The Soviet experience since April 1985 provides clues to the potential costs of reform. When implemented "from the top," the first reforms brought light to numerous problems that had accumulated in the country for decades. An attempt was made to address these problems by creating new democratic institutions in economics and politics. These institutions, however, proved insufficient. Moreover, the governing bodies were not prepared to confront society's most vital problems and proved unable to contain the struggle for political power within a framework of law and civilized conduct. As a result, the search for a resolution of the crisis led to one dead end after another. The operating principle became "every man for himself," and separatist movements became stronger.

Several processes accelerated simultaneously: Ethnic conflicts grew acute, the economic crisis worsened, and efforts were made to form a new system of political democracy in the center and the republics. Interaction among these developments fueled conflict in all three areas, even as advocates of reform made extraordinary efforts to contain these processes peacefully.

Events up to April 1991 showed the center and republics that without the participation of key actors it would prove impossible to cope with real and urgent problems. The outline of a policy of "social agreement" thus began to take shape, and a general platform for interrepublic cooperation emerged.

The Nine-Plus-One Agreement marked a turning point. It creates a basis for implementing a unified concept of economic and political transformation in nine republics that make up 90 percent of the country's territory. The realization that each republic's particular problems stemmed from common causes created the basis for more constructive interaction.

The process of democratization continues. President Gorbachev's declarations show how determined he and other leaders are to implement substantive steps to build consensus among all political groups in the USSR, to carry out radical economic reforms, and to cooperate with the advanced industrial nations. The first-ever presidential elections of Russia have been held. Despite serious deficiencies in its economic reform program, the Soviet government is thus on a politically sound course, adapting its policies to accommodate the interests of the republics.

Analysis of economic developments in the Soviet Union during the last six months, however, suggests that because of a serious recession in industry and growing inflation, the economy is quickly losing its internal capacity to implement decisive reforms by itself. If the USSR chooses an isolationist path to transformation, the ensuing pain will become so intense that the necessary reforms may prove impossible to carry out. These dangers are further compounded by the fact that the country is a military superpower.

Given the complexity and difficulties of the internal situation in the USSR, why does the serious reform have any chance of success? The answer lies in objective developments that show that the society is now prepared for radical transformation in both economics and politics.

Attempts to solve the country's problems within the framework of old ideological dogmas and by means of inconsistent reforms and the use of force have made the situation much worse. The futility of current political cliches and economic methods has been clearly demonstrated to the populace. The need for decisive measures to overcome the impasse is clear to all.

The results are:

1. The strengthening of views on reform and the clarification of the goals and tasks that now confront the reformers, as shown by:

- The recognition of the tight linkage between progress in economic reform and democratization of political institutions

- The definition of the most important tasks in the near-term: radical economic reform, the building of social consensus, and the formation of a strong coalition that could effectively resist those forces not interested in reform

- The understanding of the need for widespread dissemination and popular acceptance of the ideas of a market economy, including private ownership, price liberalization, and structural adjustments

- The creation of the basis for conducting wide-ranging negotiations on the issue of redefining the legitimate powers of the center, both legislative and executive. Having learned from the experience of economic agreements in the fall of 1990 and the acuteness of current problems, the parties, which include all interested participants, may complete this complex process in a relatively short time

- The rejection of the command structure of the economy, and appreciation of the need for new management structures

- The implementation of major changes in foreign policy: the withdrawal of Soviet troops from Eastern Europe, the beginning of genuine reductions in armaments and defense expenditures, discrediting the idea of an external enemy, a new attitude of openness to the world economy, an understanding of the need to integrate the country into world civilization, and an agreement in principle on granting full sovereignty to the Baltic states

2. A significant broadening of the popular support for reform, including:

• Participation of broad segments of the populace in the reform process and the recognition of their personal interests in this process and of the need to satisfy those interests

• Emergence of an entrepreneurial sector, changes in behavior and attitudes, and the creation of market structures

• Growth in political activity and in citizens' demands on office-holders

3. A growing pragmatism and a sense of urgency for action, manifested in:

• A decline in the standard of living and a growing sense of disorientation strengthening a resolve for action

• The necessity to maintain public trust pressuring those in power to seek to improve the situation in the shortest possible time

• A sharp deterioration of the economic situation resulting in immediate steps taken for stabilization

A precise recognition of the goals and problems of societal transformation, the choice of a market economy and democracy, the popular support for reform, and a growing resolve for immediate action—all these mean that in the present situation, a comprehensive reform program supported by the advanced industrialized democracies could rally all reform-oriented forces.

Now the moment of truth has arrived: a unique moment for unprecedented cooperation inside the Soviet Union and between the Soviet Union and the West. Today there exists a chance for the resources and talent of the USSR to become a pillar of order rather than disorder in the world. This is a historic opportunity in the life of a great nation. The decisions taken now will shape the fate of future generations.

3
WHAT ARE
THE WEST'S STAKES
IN THE SOVIET FUTURE?

There is a view that the West should sit on the sidelines, leaving the Soviet Union to stagnate or even collapse. This view reveals a profound lack of historical perspective. Economic chaos after World War I bred extremism in which Nazism took root and brought Hitler to power. The interwar economic blizzard toppled new democracies in Eastern Europe in favor of authoritarian regimes.

This view also betrays a lack of imagination about what a free and democratic Soviet Union would mean for the West. Western nations spend more than $250 billion annually defending themselves against Soviet military threats. Economic and political reform in the USSR that sharply reduced such threats would create the opportunity to realize a significant peace dividend. In economic terms, investments in successful transformation would pay a high rate of return. And the benefits to Western security of a world in which the West's fears of Soviet nuclear missiles were no greater than current fears of other nation's nuclear weapons cannot be measured in dollars alone.

The array of Western stakes in the future of the Soviet Union includes security, economic, political, environmental, and human interests. Among these, the West's preeminent goal must continue to be to avoid a nuclear war in which it would be among the first victims. Although the likelihood of a deliberate nuclear exchange has declined, the consequences of a failure of deterrence are so great that this issue must continue to top any list of Western vital interests vis-a-vis the Soviet Union. Further decline in the risk of nuclear war will occur with the successful negotiation of START and the institutionalization of a cooperative relationship. Should the process of reform in the Soviet Union fail and a dictator seize power, however, the risks of nuclear war could rise sufficiently to dominate Western attention once again.

This canonical nuclear threat is now rivalled by a second, almost equally terrifying prospect: the disintegration of the Soviet Union into chaos and civil wars. No single event in the postwar period would present such high and uncontrollable risks of nuclear war as the violent collapse of the Soviet Union. Under such conditions, what prospects would there be for centralized command and control of the Soviet Union's 30,000 nuclear warheads? In the case of a Soviet "Lebanonization," would nuclear artillery shells and other advanced conventional weapons become available in international arms bazaars for terrorists or dictatorial states? If nuclear weapons fell into the hands of warring republics, violence could spread.

A related risk is posed by prospects of additional Chernobyls. With fifty civilian nuclear power reactors across the Soviet Union and scores of research reactors in scientific institutes, it is easy to imagine a tragic intersection between civil violence and a nuclear facility.

The size, capabilities, and location of Soviet military forces matter to the West. The United States and its Western allies thus have a profound interest in whether the Soviet Union, even under conditions of severe economic hardship, eventually begins a new round of force modernization or pursues further force reductions, either unilaterally or through arms control agreements. These factors are important both because of the risks they represent, and because of their impact on Western defense spending and the size of American forces that should prudently remain in Europe. A breakup of the Soviet Union and fragmentation of its enormous military force into civil wars among components would pose unprecedented defense challenges for Washington and its NATO allies.

In assessing Western interests, it is necessary to recognize that for the foreseeable future the Soviet army will continue to be the largest and most powerful in Europe. Whatever future the Soviet Union and republics choose, these military forces will retain their historic role in defending Russia and the Soviet Union against outside invaders. But the special role in Soviet society to be played by the military will be significantly affected by the kind of society the Soviet Union becomes. In a democratic Soviet Union of voluntary republics, the army's special role would more closely resemble that of military forces in the democracies of the West.

As it has in the past, the Soviet Union will continue to pursue a foreign policy that serves its own interests. The question is: what policy, in what interests? As former President Nixon has argued recently: "The security of one nuclear superpower cannot be built on the insecurity of the other. We need the USSR as a reliable international partner in building a new world order."

Will Moscow be a partner with the West in trying to help manage the emergence of an independent and peaceful Eastern Europe, or will Soviet actions and events add to the inherent instability of that region? Will Soviet new thinking extend to Asia, particularly to Soviet-Japanese relations? Will the Soviet government continue its cooperation with the West to ameliorate internal and regional conflicts, to build a more stable Mideast after the Gulf War? Will the West and the USSR proceed in concert to slow the flow of nuclear, chemical, biological, and ballistic missile technology to unstable parts of the world, in particular to the Middle East and South Asia? For all these issues and many others, the peaceful transformation of the Soviet Union offers the best prospects for the continuation of the present course of foreign policy set by the Soviet leadership.

Given its geopolitical position, developments in the Soviet Union inevitably affect neighbors not only to its west but to its south and east. With 60 million Moslems living within Soviet borders, the Soviet Union can play a special role in moderating the radical inclinations of fundamentalists, including terrorists. Recent Soviet-Western cooperation has made possible the resolution of regional conflicts around the globe as shown in Angola, Cambodia, Central America, and Afghanistan.

The West will also be affected by Soviet environmental practices and policies. With its current antiquated industrial plants, the Soviet Union is one of the world's leading polluters and contributors to global warming. Reform promises to reduce the Soviet contribution to global pollution; without reform, pollution will increase.

Soviet economic developments will affect Western economic interests. The Soviet Union has vast natural resources and is the largest producer of the most valuable minerals. As the producer of one-fifth of the world's daily oil output, the Soviet Union has the potential to contribute significantly to the diversity, reliability, and stability of world energy supplies. Recent events in the Gulf provide a sharp reminder that the region on which the world depends for critical energy supplies is highly unstable. While Soviet energy production is currently declining, as are exports, no country has a greater potential to increase energy exports through the application of modern technology and incentives to production, as well as the management of domestic conservation.

The Soviet Union's human potential in natural scientists, engineers, mathematicians, and technicians is among the greatest in the world. Soviet achievements in space, in selected areas of technology, and in defense are well-known. The application of these people and technologies to nonmilitary purposes could not only improve standards of living in the Soviet Union but contribute to the world economy.

Conversely, if the disintegration of the Soviet economy proceeds unabated, the impact on the countries of Eastern Europe and other Soviet trading partners could be severe. With the dissolution of COMECON and the accompanying shift to trade on the basis of world prices, trade between the Soviet Union and Eastern Europe has collapsed. The cost to enterprises that were previously oriented to Soviet markets, as well as to Soviet enterprises dependent upon Eastern European inputs, is a major factor affecting the prospects for Eastern European economies today. The success of reforms in Eastern Europe could therefore be greatly enhanced by a successful Soviet program for moving rapidly to the market economy.

Thus the West has notable security, political, and potential economic stakes in the Soviet Union's future. But real interests do not end there. The principal reason why Soviet reform efforts strike such sympathetic notes in the West is not promised slow-downs in Soviet tank production, although that is surely welcome. Rather, most citizens in the West respond because *glasnost* and institutional change within the Soviet Union seem to reflect common values. The prospect of nearly 300 million more human beings having the opportunity to enjoy the freedoms of a democracy and the prosperity of a market economy must be in the West's enduring interests. The integration into the world community of peoples with such a rich history and culture, and such intellectual potential, would be an event of historic significance.

Given the West's stakes in the Soviet future, Western leaders must make a choice. The West shares with the Soviet Union a common physical and political space. It can provide assistance to the Soviet Union in its march down the road to freedom. Or it can attempt to sit on the sidelines. But what it cannot do is escape a game in which its vital interests are at stake.

4

A PROGRAM FOR POLITICAL AND ECONOMIC TRANSFORMATION

POLITICAL TRANSFORMATION

Without economic reform, there cannot be sustainable political reform. Without political reform, there cannot be effective economic reform. The two must go hand in hand.

The Soviet Union has already made important strides toward democracy. It has held free elections at republic and local levels, abolished the Communist Party's constitutional monopoly on power, and adopted legal guarantees of freedom of the press, freedom of religion, freedom of expression, and freedom of emigration.

A number of the powers and responsibilities of the

center have already been devolved onto the republics, and the powers of local governments have been increased. The draft Union Treaty provides for a significant expansion of the powers of the republics and a voluntary assignment to the central government of specific responsibilities for defense, national transportation, and energy supply and nuclear power generation.

The Soviet political system is gradually moving toward a separation of powers. The free press is playing an ever-greater role in the political process. The most important decisions are increasingly being reached through democratic and legal procedures. But the transition from a totalitarian to a democratic system of government is creating new problems, notably that of increased ethnic conflict. Every step of the way meets resistance, making it difficult to proceed.

The historic Nine-Plus-One Agreement between President Gorbachev and the leaders of nine republics ushered in a new era of political reform. Without this agreement, the Soviet Union would no doubt be confronting further civil strife and economic chaos. The leaders agreed on a plan that sets out the objective conditions under which democracy can flourish and economic reform can succeed. The plan includes:

- Completion of work on a new draft Union Treaty among sovereign republics

- Preparation and adoption of a new constitution for the union within six months of the treaty's signing

- Election of new "union power bodies," both legislative and executive, following the adoption of the constitution

- Recognition of the sovereignty of all republics, including the right to decide freely whether or not to join the union

- A ban on ethnic discrimination

The plan will establish a new union on the basis of voluntary membership, equality, and the protection of human rights. It thus reverses the trend toward disintegration and moves affirmatively toward the creation of a democratic government. Only such a government, which commands the support of its people, will have the capacity to implement an effective economic reform program.

Words are helpful. Actions are decisive. The Nine-Plus-One Agreement points the way to a coherent, sequenced program and timetable. Milestones in democratization should include:

- June 12, 1991: first-ever popular election of the president of the Russian republic (now accomplished)

- End of summer 1991: signing of the Union Treaty by at least nine republics and possibly more. The treaty will legitimize the devolution of powers from the center to the republics, reallocate governmental responsibilities at all levels, and set out procedures for establishing new federal governing institutions

- Fall of 1991: signing of an Economic Union Agreement among both the signatories of the Union Treaty and those republics that choose not to join the union

- Fall of 1991: negotiations with republics that have chosen not to join the Economic Union concerning trade and currency, the sharing of the Soviet Union's internal and external debt, the status of military bases, defense industries, and industries of national significance, and guarantees of the rights of ethnic minorities

- Summer of 1991: initiation by the union and republic governments of negotiations involving all parties to resolve ethnic conflicts and limit the use of force

- Summer of 1991: legal recognition of labor organizations and negotiations on strikes, wage increases, and potential layoffs

- Spring of 1992: adoption of the new constitution of the USSR, based on the Union Treaty and the Economic Union Agreement

- Summer of 1992: holding of free multiparty elections to the federal legislature, and reorganization of union executive organization

Fulfilling these steps will provide hard evidence that the process of political transformation is proceeding decisively toward democracy. Such steps constitute a critical condition for the successful strategic interaction between the Soviet Union and the West. Objectively, economic reform will follow only under these conditions, since such reform is crucial to the effective utilization of Western economic assistance.

Democracy is a process, not a static condition. The Soviet Union will not become democratic overnight, but it will move unambiguously toward that goal by fully carrying out the commitments made in the Nine-Plus-One Agreement. By replacing confrontation with the process of consensus-building, union and republican leaders are now giving reforms a real chance.

ECONOMIC TRANSFORMATION

Transformation of the current Soviet economy will require a breakthrough as distinct from the economic policies of the past six years as the transformation to "new thinking" in Soviet international relations was from what preceded it. The lesson of Eastern European economic reform in the 1980s is that partial reform focused on decentralization of economic decision-making or on macroeconomic stabilization will fail in the absence of positive incentives that come from private ownership and competition. Reform programs aimed at adjusting a centrally controlled and directed system by merely tilting toward the market are doomed to fail. Success requires that leaders understand that transformation means the death of the old system and the birth of an entirely new system.

The union and republican governments have agreed in principle to the major elements necessary for the transformation to a market economy: stabilization, liberalization, privatization, and integration into the world economy. All that is lacking is a coherent, feasible program for achieving these goals. Our purpose in this section is to outline such a program, one that could be implemented successfully over the next several years with significant Western assistance.

The urgency for economic reform is now dictated by the accelerating collapse of the Soviet economy. Output is plummeting, while open inflation has reached 100 percent per year and the budget and balance of payments deficits are mounting. The economy has broken loose from a seventy-year-old command apparatus. In the absence of macroeconomic discipline and radical structural reforms, the country faces a period of protracted hyperinflation accompanied by sharp declines in output. This will intensify political instability and could lead to collapse. The return to a centralized economy is not only unwanted, but is not possible. Radical economic reform offers the only viable alternative. Therefore, in concert with the necessary political prerequisites (including the Union Treaty and the Economic Union Agreement), comprehensive economic reform must be rapidly initiated.

The goal of the program of economic transformation is to create a *normal market economy* in the Soviet Union in the shortest possible time. Experience in other countries and economic logic dictate that the reforms must be rapid and comprehensive to have a chance of success. The reforms must also be uncompromising, in the sense that they must aim to create an economy whose fundamental features will resemble those of the advanced industrial economies. The pattern of private and public ownership of enterprises and land should be comparable to that of the West, and the trade and financial systems should be integrated closely into the world economy.

The program can best be described by its targets at the end of 1997. The program envisions a financially stable economy then, with an ownership pattern similar to that of Western Europe. It envisions an economy integrated into world trading relations, and using generally accepted methods for regulating transnational flows of goods, capital, and services. These steps will begin to narrow the growing gap between the living standards of Soviet citizens and the living standards of the advanced industrial economies.

The successful strategy for transformation to a normal

market economy must be built with six basic elements. These are clear in international experience, and are embodied in the IMF-World Bank-OECD-EBRD *The Economy of the USSR,* as well as the earlier Soviet "500 Day" plan. The six include:

- *Stabilization* of the macroeconomy, which means sharply reducing governmental budget deficits and curbing monetary and credit excesses. Eliminating these deficits will necessitate sharp cuts in defense expenditures, and in subsidies to military enterprises and other state industries. It will also mean an end to printing money in excess of real growth and a sharp shrinkage of credit expansion.

- *Liberalization* of prices so that market forces of supply and demand determine prices, production, and consumption

- *Firmly establishing private property,* including agricultural, guaranteed by a legal system that protects rights of ownership and enforces contracts

- *Privatization* of enterprise, including legalization of entrepreneurship in creating new enterprises, sale of most state enterprises, and the demonopolization of large state industries

- *Opening the economy,* including free trade, appropriate protection for foreign investment, opportunities for repatriation of profits, and convertibility of the ruble

- *Limiting direct governmental intervention in the economy.* Success in economic reform will require a complete reorientation in the role of government. This means withdrawal from the command system and an end to the economic functions that government agencies have performed in the command economy: state orders for most goods, state decisions about most investments, state determination of most prices, and so forth. Instead, in a market economy, government has the essential but limited economic role of creating the legal and economic framework of a market in which private citizens and private enterprises play the decisive role. This includes protecting and enforcing rights of property and contract, fostering competitive markets by means of antimonopoly regulations, maintaining sound fiscal and monetary policies, developing a social safety net, and ensuring the development of an essential infrastructure, including education, transportation, and communication.

Each nation has unique historical and cultural characteristics that lead to distinct economic institutions. There are differences between European Community commercial law and U.S. law; between ownership patterns in Germany and those in the United Kingdom; between financial institutions and practices in Japan and France. A market economy in the Soviet Union will also reflect special features of that nation's past. The Soviet solution will be uniquely its own—not a forced fit into a U.S., Swedish, or German model.

Nonetheless, recognition of historical and cultural identity should not be allowed to raise illusions about the possibility of some "third way." The Soviet Union's unambiguous objective must be to create as rapidly as possible a market economy with the commonly shared basic characteristics of the advanced industrial democracies.

In applying these principles to design a strategy for

Soviet economic transformation, it is necessary to begin with an appreciation that the Soviet Union is not Eastern Europe. Special features of the Soviet Union's case include not only the distress described earlier, but great strengths that can be mobilized in the transformation:

- Soviet citizens rank among the world's most accomplished mathematicians, scientists, and engineers (not to mention chess players). These individuals constitute the largest reserve of highly educated and trained talent outside the most advanced industrial countries.

- In areas where the Soviet Union has chosen to specialize, as, for example, in satellite launches, fighter aircraft, other defense technologies, lasers, and some areas of medicine, it is among the world leaders.

- Having permitted virtually no private property, the Soviet Union can now make a significant, immediate improvement in people's lives by simply allowing them to own private property, including land.

- Having almost no middle class, it can again offer opportunities for rapid increases in productivity by just letting go and allowing private entrepreneurship to express itself.

- Having had the most legally restrictive environment for private initiative, its relaxation of these legal constraints should, in particular, produce rapid increases in the supply of items like food as farms are privatized, and in service and retail enterprises as the legal and economic environment becomes hospitable to them.

- Soviet reserves rank in the top three in virtually every valuable natural resource. The command economy's method of exploiting these natural resources has

37

caused untold environmental devastation. By failing to use the most appropriate technologies, current Soviet natural resource extraction recovers less than half of the resources extracted by international equivalents. Introduction of appropriate technology should therefore not only rapidly increase supplies but also reduce negative environmental effects. Increases in prices for natural resources will lead to more efficient domestic utilization and therefore declining domestic demand.

- As economic circumstances have worsened, the Soviet people have been forced to become self-reliant simply to survive. The degree of ingenuity and entrepreneurship that goes into finding the necessities of life, and the practices of barter in gray markets that all citizens deal with everyday, have encouraged behavior that will, when legalized in the normal market conditions, produce surplus for other consumers.

The program outlined here seeks to utilize these resources by focusing early and fast on the essential actions that must be taken to transform seven decades of malpractice into a basic market economy. Over the first 18 months the program will establish a framework that will then attract private investment, both domestic and international, in ways that support reform rather than bolster the old command system.

Broadly speaking, the plan presented here divides the transformation process into two periods. In the first period (1991 to 1993), the legal and economic institutions of the market economy are created and a considerable portion of state property is transformed into private property. In the second period (1994 to 1997), the transformation process focuses on structural adjustment in the economy, accelerating the shifts from public to private ownership, from military to civilian industry, from heavy industry to production of consumer goods and services, and from a closed economy to an open economy.

In the remainder of this chapter, we describe the reform program in more detail. The essential elements are summarized in Table 1, which sets out the key Soviet actions and Western responses. Table 2 (at the end of the chapter) demonstrates how the reform program deals with the specific problems now confronting the Soviet economy. Table 3 (also at the end of the chapter) highlights comparisons between the proposed reform and the command system it replaces.

PHASE ONE
Creation of the Legal and Economic Framework for a Market Economy (1991–93)

The objectives of the first period will be tackled in three stages:

1. Institution building: June 1991–early 1992
2. Macroeconomic stabilization and market reform: 1992
3. Consolidation of stabilization, intensification of privatization, and beginning of structural reforms: 1993

Stage 1. Institution Building (June 1991–Early 1992)

The strategic priorities of Stage 1 are fourfold:

• Continue the development of the political framework required for a market economy. This will include the negotiation of major union/republic treaties to guar-

Table 1
KEY ACTIONS IN SOVIET ECONOMIC REFORM

PHASE ONE: *Creation of the Legal and Economic Framework (1991–1993)*

Stage 1: Institution Building (June 1991–Early 1992)

SOVIET ACTIONS

- All-Union Treaty
- Economic Union Agreement, including setting up of IEC (Inter-Republican Economic Commission)
- Implementation of small-scale privatization
- Price liberalization
- Movement toward unified exchange rates
- Cooperation with international agencies group to examine recent and proposed Soviet economic laws and to propose changes and new laws, which are to be enacted by relevant legislative bodies
- Elimination of remaining restrictions and particularly criminal statues on private economic activity and market behavior
- Conclusion of bilateral agreements on guarantees for foreign investment
- Freeze on new social spending programs at all governmental levels
- Reduction of enterprise subsidies
- Devolution of privatization responsibility to the republics where smaller scale will allow greater speed
- Land reform measures

WESTERN RESPONSES

- Associate Membership in IMF and World Bank, discussions of reform and assistance programs with international partners, technical assistance begins
- Food and medical aid begins to flow as program progresses
- Provision of technical assistance
- Trade liberalization measures as provided to Eastern Europe

Table 1 *(continued)*

Stage 2: Macroeconomic Stabilization and Market Reforms (1992)

SOVIET ACTIONS

- New Union constitution in spring 1992
- Open, multiparty elections for legislatures in summer 1992
- Stabilization and liberalization program put into effect
- Budget balanced through sharp reductions in subsidies, foreign aid, and military spending
- Elimination of price controls with small list of exceptions
- Independent central bank set up on Federal Reserve lines
- Current account convertibility achieved
- Liberalization of international trade
- Elimination of all restrictions on private economic transactions
- Accelerated small-scale privatization
- Improved enforcement of contract law and commercial codes
- Liberalization of agricultural markets
- Solicitation of foreign direct investment for development of energy and natural resources
- Food stamp program instituted to cushion potential social costs of price liberalization

PROPOSED WESTERN RESPONSE

- Membership in IMF and World Bank
- Large scale financial aid begins, led by the IMF, and conditional on implementation of the reform program
- Intensive technical assistance, in support of ongoing and planned reforms

Table 1 *(continued)*

Stage 3: Consolidation of Stabilization, Large-Scale Privatization, and Beginning of Structural Reforms (1993)

SOVIET ACTIONS

- Maintenance of strict macroeconomic control
- Defense industry conversion accelerates
- Preparations for privatization of large firms and initial privatizations, continuation of small-scale privatization, active implementation of anti-monopoly policies
- Land reform proceeds
- Financial market infrastructure develops, with emphasis on banks
- Infrastructure projects get under way, including transport and communications, where possible with international private sector involvement
- Agricultural markets expand
- Upgrading of technology and capital stock, with international private sector involvement

PROPOSED WESTERN RESPONSE

- Foreign assistance continues, conditional on implementation of reform program

PHASE TWO: *Intensification of Structural Reforms (1994–1997)*

SOVIET ACTIONS

- Privatization of large-scale industry intensified
- Defense industry conversion intensifies
- Consumer goods and services sectors expand, heavy industry contracts
- Housing privatization intensifies
- Fiscal reform implemented
- Labor markets liberalized
- International private investment expands

PROPOSED WESTERN RESPONSE

- Official foreign assistance decreases

antee a unified market and a clear division of governmental responsibilities, agreements with international institutions such as the IMF, World Bank and EBRD and agreements with Western governments.

- Continue the development of the legal framework required for the market economy including legislation on contract and corporate law and removal of limitations on private economic activity.

- Prepare for a full program of macroeconomic stabilization through such measures as controls on social spending and government credit.

- Implement privatization and liberalization programs that will maintain the momentum of reform and ease macroeconomic pressures. These include privatization of small retail establishments, trucks, cars and some agricultural land and liberalization of prices for categories including luxury goods and consumer goods.

DETAILED DESCRIPTION

The necessary political agreements among the republics, and between the republics and the union government will be reached by the end of 1991. Agreements on cooperation between the USSR and the advanced industrial countries, and the USSR and the international financial institutions, will be developed and adopted. Legal, economic, and institutional preparations will be made for the stabilization and liberalization program that will be introduced at the start of 1992.

Two essential political agreements have to be reached

in this period: a Union Treaty and an Economic Union Agreement. These two agreements will re-create a unified market throughout the union and establish the fundamental economic framework within which Western aid can proceed. Features of the unified market will include:

- A single currency in the territory of the Economic Union that will be the sole legal tender

- A single monetary policy set by an independent central bank

- Coordination of budget policies among the republics, and between the republics and the Union government

- Elimination of internal customs barriers and the adoption of a uniform customs policy toward the rest of the world

- A common trade policy toward the nonparticipating republics

- Common economic legislation

- A negotiated set of minimal social policies that will apply throughout the entire economic space.

Features of the framework will include:

- An Economic Union Agreement that will designate sources of fiscal revenue for the governments at various levels and assign clear responsibilities for budgetary outlays. The Union government will have independent sources of revenue. The Economic Union Agreement will provide for coordinated budgetary policies among the republics and the Union government in order to eliminate budget deficits (including extra-budgetary funds).

- The USSR State Bank reorganized along the lines of the Federal Reserve System, uniting the republic-level central banks into an institution that will carry out a single monetary policy. The governing board of this Council of Central Banks will be established in the summer of 1991.

- Economic policy in areas other than fiscal, monetary and trade policy (privatization, agricultural and housing reform, etc.) determined mainly by the republic governments, with the center helping to coordinate. Responsibility for economic legislation will be divided between the union and republic governments in accordance with the agreed upon division of power in managing the economy. If the laws of a republic contradict the union laws in an area where authority is delegated to the union, the union legislation will prevail and vice versa.

- An Inter-Republican Economic Commission (IEC) will be established as an executive body for the Economic Union. This commission will be headed by the Prime Minister of the USSR, with representatives from each of the republics. The precise structure of the IEC and other executive bodies at the union level will be determined in the Union Treaty and the Economic Union Agreement. It will have the following functions:

- To develop a common stabilization and liberalization policy for the unified market

- To prepare a detailed economic reform program in conjunction with the international institutions

- To assume oversight responsibility for the implementation of the program of economic transformation

Representatives from the republics will participate in the preparation of the transition program. After the program has been prepared, it will be submitted to the union government and the Supreme Soviet for approval. The major principles of the program will be ratified by the parliaments of the union and the individual republics.

Development of a new legal framework will proceed on several fronts. Laws on banks, banking and currency market regulations, new customs codes, emigration law and a number of other necessary economic components have already been adopted. Laws on foreign investments and equities are in the process of being adopted. In the second half of 1991, all existing and planned economic legislation will be reviewed by the IEC in cooperation with Western institutions. The focus will be on the core economic laws: contract law, corporate law, investment law, foreign investment law, foreign exchange law, fiscal and customs legislation, labor legislation, and environmental law. On the basis of this work, appropriate legal changes and new laws will be passed by the relevant parliaments.

Before introducing a complete stabilization program early in 1992, a number of preparatory economic measures will be implemented:

- A reduction of subsidies linked to continuing liberalization of prices during the last part of 1991

- A freeze on the adoption of new social-spending programs at the union and republic levels, and a consolidation of the existing programs until new programs can be incorporated in balanced budgets on the basis of the new Economic Union Treaty

- Cuts in other budgetary expenditures for the second half of 1991, based on new emergency budgets to be adopted by the republics and the union

- Operational limits on the credits granted to enterprises

- Legal restrictions on the extension of credit by the State Bank of the USSR to the Union and republic governments and to the central banks of the republics for the purpose of financing budgetary deficits

The initial steps and preparation for full liberalization will include:

- Rapid liberalization of prices of broad categories of luxury goods and consumer durables

- A narrowing of the gap between the commercial exchange rate and the market exchange rate to be achieved through changes in the commercial exchange rate

- Measures to develop the market for foreign exchange, including an elimination of the restrictions on personal holdings of foreign currency, measures to increase the availability of foreign exchange to enterprises at market prices, and preparations for a unified foreign exchange market within the Soviet Union

- An increase in the foreign exchange retention quotas (the foreign exchange that may be retained by exporters), and, conversely, a reduction in mandatory foreign exchange payments by enterprises to the state

- Adoption and initial implementation of legislation for the rapid privatization of small-scale enterprises and physical assets (e.g., retail shops, restaurants, trucks)

- Adoption of legislation for privatizing large-scale enterprises and/or establishing agencies at the union and republic levels to hold the government's shares and to formulate and implement a privatization program beginning in 1992

- Continuation of land reform measures including further redistribution of land in favor of private farms, land assessment, introduction of a land tax, organization of Land Bank. During 1991, approximately five million hectares will be distributed to the populace to increase the amount of private, supplementary cultivation, and to support the creation of horticultural cooperatives and associations.

- Partial indexing of incomes during the second half of 1991

- Establishment of unemployment insurance funds and of labor registry offices throughout the country

- Introduction of measures to reorganize the statistical system to make it consistent with standard international practices (to be carried out in collaboration with the international financial institutions and the statistical offices of the European Community)

- Elimination of all remaining restrictions (particularly criminal statutes) on normal private economic activity and private market behavior

The following international initiatives should be taken during this institution-building stage:

First, there is a need to prepare the Soviet Union for entry into international financial institutions. The USSR should be offered immediate associate membership in the International Monetary Fund and the World Bank, and should be granted the opportunity of achieving full membership beginning January 1, 1992. This special status would allow the Soviet Union to begin receiving large-scale technical assistance and to prepare the documents and actions necessary for full membership. Current limitations on EBRD lending to the Soviet Union should be modified as of January 1, 1992 in order to allow for the necessary lending to the emerging private sector. Technical missions should be organized to conduct negotiations for loan programs that will come into effect early in 1992 when the Soviet Union receives full membership in the IMF and World Bank. The West will have to develop a mechanism to coordinate financial and technical assistance to the Soviet Union.

Second, negotiations should be initiated on trade agreements to remove trade barriers between the Soviet Union and the West. The Soviet Union should prepare for a nearly complete liberalization of trade in 1992, including the elimination of most licensing and quantitative restrictions, the introduction of currency convertibility, and the introduction of low and nearly uniform tariffs. On the basis of the newly passed emigration law and (if necessary) its extension, the U.S. should grant the Soviet Union Most-Favored-Nation (MFN) status and ratify and implement the Bilateral Investment Treaty before the end of 1991. The European Community has already committed itself to extend the same trade access to the Soviet Union after the rest of Eastern Europe. A phased program of shrinking COCOM restrictions on the export of high-technology products to the Soviet Union should be implemented. Soviet legislation on foreign investment and bilateral agreements on guarantees for foreign investors would also be implemented.

Finally, Western economic assistance should include supplies of medicine and food to prepare for price liberalization, particularly in the agricultural and consumer markets. Most of these supplies would be held in reserve stocks until the beginning of 1992, when they will be used to intervene in commodity markets to help stabilize prices and supplies at the outset of commodity market liberalization.

Stage 2. Macroeconomic Stabilization and Market Reforms (1992)

As the implementation of the Stage 1 initiatives continues, Stage 2 will focus on three new priorities:

- A full program of macroeconomic stabilization including the creation of an independent central bank and a balanced budget

- Large-scale price liberalization, supported by Western aid, extending to all but a small group of essential consumer goods

- The opening of the economy with Western support, including the removal of trade barriers, the encouragement of foreign investment, and the creation of a convertible ruble

DETAILED DESCRIPTION

In the spring of 1992, a new USSR Constitution based on the Union Treaty and the Economic Union Agreement will be adopted. This Constitution will further democratize the political structure, decentralize power by delineating functions for each level of government, and set out a new structure of governmental powers and responsibilities at the union level. In the summer of 1992 free, multiparty elections will be conducted for legislative bodies of the union, and a reorganization of the union executive institutions will be completed.

The program of economic stabilization and liberalization will aim to eliminate financial imbalances and inflationary pressures, establish prices on the basis of supply and demand, and create an open international trading system by making the ruble convertible and substantially eliminating administrative and tariff barriers to trade. The centerpiece of the program will be a set of budgetary and financial measures, combined with the elimination of administrative controls over prices of most products and the devaluation of the commercial rate of the ruble aimed at making the ruble convertible. The program will go into effect early in 1992. The exact timing will depend on the actions that have been taken at the end of 1991, which will in turn depend on the nature of Western involvement and assistance up to that point.

Balanced government finances, including the budget and extrabudgetary funds, will be achieved through a combination of cuts in expenditures and increases in government revenues. There will be a prohibition on financing government expenses by central bank credits. The use of extrabudgetary funds to finance the government will be severely restricted. Government spending will be reduced through the elimination of nearly all subsidies, and through cuts in defense expenditures, foreign aid, etc. As overall defense outlays fall, the structure of defense spending will change. Less will be spent on arms acquisitions, and more for the maintenance of the army and the social infrastructure for military personnel. Subsidies, coupons, and rationing will continue for only a few vital consumer goods (bread, milk, vegetable oil and butter, sugar, medicines, mass transit fees, apartment rents, and public services). These measures will reduce government subsidies provided through the budget by several percent of GNP. The share of social spending in the budget and in the country's GNP will be lowered. New tax legislation will be introduced to achieve a broad-based tax system with low marginal rates of taxation. The range of goods covered by a turnover tax will be broadened and the range of rates of turnover taxes will be narrowed thus preparing the way for a value added tax. The system of royalty payments on natural resources will be rationalized.

The independence of the central banking system from the government will be achieved through a new central bank law. The central bank will severely limit the growth of, or actually reduce, the supply of money in circulation. The central bank will rely on market mechanisms for monetary control, such as open-market operations, required reserve ratios for commercial banks, and refinancing operations of commercial banks, rather than on direct administrative controls on credit activity. The current activities of specialized government banks will be transferred to the commercial banking sector.

The elimination of administrative controls over all aspects of pricing will also occur early in 1992, in coordination with the provision of international support. Exceptions to complete price liberalization will be few and specific. In addition to the remaining consumer subsidies on vital commodities, administrative price limits will remain on several basic energy resources and on some types of transport fees. Energy prices will be kept substantially below world prices at the outset of the economic program. This gap will be closed during a three-year adjustment period. The difference between world and internal prices will be managed through a system of export and import taxes. The liberalization of prices will occur on a synchronized basis in all the republics. The jump in prices at the moment of liberalization will be moderated by the supply of goods available in government reserves. These reserves will be augmented by international balance of payments support.

Current account convertibility (or internal convertibility) of the ruble (that is, convertibility for trade and most other current account transactions) will be established, based on an adequate devaluation of the commercial rate to a new sustainable level. Currently, the market rate of the ruble (the currency auction) is fifteen times the fixed commercial rate. In stage 1 this discrepancy will be significantly reduced through a tight credit policy, combined with a series of devaluations of the ruble's commercial exchange rate, and an increase in the volume of hard currency sales by the government on the internal market. With the beginning of the program of macroeconomic stabilization, it will be eliminated.

The convertibility and stability of the value of the ruble will be supported by consistent monetary policies adopted by the independent central bank, and will be strengthened by the currency stabilization fund established with the financial assistance of the advanced industrial countries. All economic agents (enterprises and citizens) will receive the right to purchase foreign currency at the commercial rate for the conduct of international trade transactions. Exporters will remit their foreign currency earnings to the Foreign Trade Bank (VneshEconomBank) at the official exchange rate. A parallel currency market for nontrade transactions will operate freely alongside the commercial foreign exchange market. The use of foreign currency for settlements of contracts within the country will, however, be forbidden.

Existing administrative limitations on external trade will be removed. Export and import licenses and quotas will be eliminated for most commodities. The export and import tax system will be substantially simplified. A system of low and nearly uniform import tariffs will be created, although the precise nature of trade restrictions will depend on the outcome of negotiations between the Soviet government and its trading partners. There will be a single regime of trade taxes which will apply to all republics in the Economic Union.

Limitations on private economic transactions will be eliminated. The enforcement of contracts, and the judicial penalties for breach of contract, will be strengthened. Limitations by republics or by the union government on the free movement of goods within the country on a commercial basis will be prohibited. Mandatory government orders will be eliminated, except for the direct procurement of military goods as stipulated in the union budget and, temporarily, a small number of goods such as pharmaceuticals. Other government purchases will be based on commercial contracts at market prices. Contracts for the supply of products for state needs will be managed by a government contract system through its own regional offices. A wide network of wholesale businesses will be developed.

The government will liberalize agricultural markets by ending administrative controls on the deliveries of foodstuffs. The systems of storage, transportation, and wholesale and retail trade of rationed goods will be privatized. A regional network of agricultural exchanges will be established. The liberalization of agricultural markets on a unionwide basis will depend, however, on an adequate governmental reserve of commodities that can be used to help stabilize the commodity markets during the initial period of liberalization. These reserve stocks will help guarantee that adequate supplies of food commodities will reach the urban population centers. Because monetary relations in the agricultural sector are so undeveloped, it will be necessary in the first few months to maintain a system of in-kind ("natural") taxation of agricultural output, but the in-kind tax rates will be kept below 15 percent of production (in contrast to the current 80 percent rate), and will be replaced by monetary taxes as soon as possible.

The nature of investment spending will change. Many state-financed programs will be stopped. Uninstalled equipment and unfinished buildings that cannot be used for production will be sold. A decrease of demand for state-sector investments due to tough financial policies and an increase in interest rates on long-term credits will allow the liberalization of prices of construction goods and should lead to an increase in private investment.

The program of financial stabilization and economic liberalization will be accompanied by the implementation of a program at all governmental levels for the acceleration of small-scale privatization. Most small-scale governmental assets will be sold at auction. The auctions will be supported by maximum public information about the assets. The responsibility for small-scale privatization will rest mainly with local government. Financial incentives for the local governments will be created to ensure fast action.

Large industrial enterprises will be reorganized as joint-stock companies or limited-liability companies as a first step toward full privatization. Initially, the equity of these enterprises will be held by Funds of State Property, established at the union and republic levels. The branch ministries and similar bodies of local government will be eliminated. While these joint-stock companies remain in state hands, the enterprises will be governed by a professional board of directors selected through a nonpolitical process. Appointments of board members will be determined by the professional qualifications of the candidates, and members of the governmental bureaucracy will not be allowed to serve, in order to reduce the chances of governmental interference in enterprise management and to avoid potential conflicts of interest.

Privatization of the large enterprises will start as rapidly as possible. The privatization process for these enterprises, however, is expected to operate on a significant scale only during the third stage, beginning in 1993. It should be recognized, however, that the privatization of large-scale enterprises will take many years to complete.

Policies for sectoral adjustment in key industrial sectors will be introduced. A special effort will be made to intensify energy exploration and development, in part through foreign direct investment. Similarly, the process of conversion of military industries to civilian use will be intensified; foreign direct investment is also expected to contribute to this process.

A variety of important social measures will be introduced. First, a system of ration coupons will be introduced for a limited number of basic foodstuffs, including bread, milk, vegetable oil, butter, and sugar. These ration coupons will allow the holder to buy a limited quantity of these commodities at a subsidized price. The free market price will apply to purchases above this amount. The costs of this subsidy system will be in the budgets of the various levels of government, and their amounts consistent with the overall budgetary balance. Second, a reform of the system of wage determination will be set in motion, to lead to free determination of wages on the basis of collective bargaining as rapidly as is feasible (though free collective bargaining will be feasible only after substantial privatization of large enterprise has been carried forward). The governmental regulation of wages will be limited to the setting of a minimum wage and, in this first phase, the use of tax mechanisms to control wage growth in state-owned enterprises.

Third, the rights of enterprises to increase and decrease the work force will be protected, and a series of social measures will be enacted to reduce the extent and burden of unemployment that may result. New pension programs and unemployment compensation payments will be established. Fourth, a program of social security will be developed for the elderly and disabled.

These stabilization and liberalization policies should be supported by wide-scale and timely international support, including:

- Establishment of a currency stabilization fund to support the convertibility of the ruble

- Balance-of-payments support in the form of foodstuffs, medicines, and cash grants and loans

- Credits to the private sector

- Investments in infrastructure and various sectors of industry

- Technical assistance

Stage 3. Consolidation of Stabilization, Large-Scale Privatization, and Beginning of Structural Reforms (1993)

Strategic priorities in Stage 3 include:

- Continuation of the initiatives of Stages 1 and 2. This will be particularly critical in the macroeconomic arena, where credit controls and balanced budgets will bankrupt many establishments.

- Privatization of large enterprises

- Conversion of portions of the defense industry into new enterprises producing nondefense goods for the Soviet market and high-technology export goods, and upgrading infrastructure. Substantial private Western involvement is anticipated.

DETAILED DESCRIPTION

Perseverance in macroeconomic stabilization will be paramount. The most important actions at this point will be the continuation of strict macroeconomic policies, including a balanced budget and restrictive credit policies of the central bank in spite of political pressures.

Small-scale privatization will continue, while the privatization of large enterprises will be broadened considerably. The focus will be on the massive sale of shares of equity of the large-scale and medium-scale state enterprises. Methods used to hasten the sale of stocks in the privatization process will include granting of favorable terms to employees of enterprises being privatized, the sale of enterprises through an installment plan, leasing, and a system of credit for buyers of state property.

To speed up the privatization process, the State Property Fund may set the book value of the enterprise below the minimum selling price level. In special cases the sale of enterprises (or of their shares) can take place at low or even symbolic prices, which can greatly increase demand. Participation rules for foreign investors in the privatization of large-scale and medium-scale enterprises will be liberalized. Other methods of privatization, such as the use of state-owned equities to help set up pension funds for industrial workers, or the privatization of shares in the form of mutual funds, will also be analyzed and implemented where useful.

At the same time, antimonopoly policy will be activated and measures will be taken to prevent consumer fraud. The development of small and medium-sized businesses will be supported through tax and credit policies. The broadening of external trade will also facilitate the formation of a competitive environment in the Soviet economy.

Starting in the second half of 1992, programs to develop the financial market infrastructure will be implemented. Specialists will be retrained, and banks and stock and commodity exchanges will be equipped with modern facilities. The technical capacity of labor registry offices, commodity exchanges, and stock markets in the republics will also be upgraded. The necessary upgrading of equipment, and the training of personnel, will be performed within the framework of programs carried out jointly with the international financial institutions.

With the support of the World Bank and the EBRD, and within the framework of agreements with the governments of the advanced industrial countries, investment projects in a number of infrastructure branches (transport, communications, telecommunications) will begin in 1993. To attract scarce international capital, a Basic Framework will be established based on best international business practice. Core principles should include: reliance on competition among international corporations to choose investment opportunities and bring to them capital, technology, and know-how, all subject to normal business risks; and government guarantees, perhaps jointly by the Soviet Union and foreign governments, against possible sovereign risk. Financial intermediaries may be created to provide loans and insurance for private investments. Such investments, licensing, and joint ventures in areas like energy, food processing, and construction will upgrade technologies and capital stock. As the economic and political situation in the country becomes more stable, the attractiveness for foreign private investment will increase. Guarantees in bilateral investment treaties and other laws will further stimulate investment.

The greatest potential for large hard currency earnings in the short term lies in the exploration, development, and export of natural resources, including energy and minerals, where investment has been plagued by uncertainties inherent in the system. The Basic Framework might be supplemented by a union entity empowered to make and implement decisions. The basic terms should be those of standard international practice, including 80–20 splits, guarantees against nationalization, rapid cost recovery to minimize the period of the risk, and a revolving credit account funded by early production to shift long guarantees back to the Soviets. With such a framework, international oil companies estimate that the Soviet Union could earn $3 billion to $5 billion by the third year of the program, and more than $15 billion annually in years 5 and beyond.

Still more pressing is the issue of the conversion of defense industry. Government grants should establish a Defense Enterprise Conversion Fund, managed by an international board modeled after the Enterprise Funds for Eastern Europe. New Soviet practices in this area should be embodied in a legal framework that encourages potential international investors and partners for joint ventures to review opportunities and to select investments. The most promising possibilities are to create new enterprises out of existing defense enterprises to produce nonmilitary products for Soviet and international markets. International corporations as well as managers of investment pools, including pension funds, have expressed great interest in investments in new nonmilitary enterprises spawned by the best of Soviet high-technology defense companies. A Defense Enterprise Conversion Fund with dollars from international governments could provide a basic insurance like OPIC to insure a percentage of private investments in such entities. With such assurances, in the context of the transformation program described here, major investment managers estimate that international investments in defense enterprise could rapidly mount to several billion dollars annually. Money from the Defense Enterprise Conversion Fund may also help support salaries and wages of employees in these enterprises while the enterprises are restructured.

For major industries that will, at least in this stage, remain monopolies of the union or republics such as electricity, telecommunications, railroads, and perhaps airlines, a combination of international technical assistance and direct support from the World Bank and EBRD should markedly improve productivity.

During this stage, enterprise insolvency problems will become more acute. Many bankruptcies may ensue. For this reason, the retraining programs for workers and civil servants, and the reorganization of public sector employment, will become particularly important.

Land reform will continue during this stage. Collective farms and state farms will be transformed into cooperatives, companies, individual farms, or other forms of enterprises with private ownership. The process of land-use redistribution and land zoning in favor of efficient economic units will be intensified. Development of a free agricultural market will facilitate the regional specialization of agricultural production and improve the efficiency of agriculture. A market for trade in land holdings will be developed on the basis of the decisions adopted by the parliaments of the republics.

Approximately one half of aid in 1993 will serve to support the country's balance of payments; the remainder will be distributed among major investment projects, such as infrastructure, the housing sector, conversion of the defense industry, and private-sector credits. Technical aid grants will continue.

Intensification of Structural Reforms (1994–1997)

By the end of the first phase of the transformation program, the infrastructure of the market system will have been built and the transportation and communications systems significantly improved. Investments in modernizing the traditional export base, including energy, will have started, and the process of modernization of technologies in such industries as agricultural processing, chemicals, pharmaceuticals and light industry will be well under way. A start will have been made on the conversion of military industry to civilian use. Investment decisions will increasingly be made on a market basis.

The priorities of the second phase of the transformation program will include:

- Intensification of changes set in process during the first phase, e.g., the structural transformation of the economy to a consumer economy, with the goal of raising the living standards of the population and achieving a positive balance of payments in the union.

- Development of the social programs required by a market economy

DETAILED DESCRIPTION

The industrial structure of the economy and of trade will change decisively during this period. The consumer goods—including consumer durables—and services sectors will expand. Heavy industries will be restructured. Production will move predominantly into the private sector. Investment will be increasingly financed by the private sector, both through domestic saving and foreign direct investment. Financial markets, including equity markets, will be developed to encourage saving and to facilitate the efficient flow of resources into investment.

Exports will expand beyond raw materials to manufactured goods. Tourism will develop. The increasing efficiency of domestic production, particularly in agriculture, will reduce imports. The trade balance will improve.

During this second phase of restructuring or structural adjustment, the government will implement several policies to support the market-led adjustment process. These include:

- Projects of industrial reconstruction, supported by the international private sector and the international financial institutions, to enable firms in specific industry sectors to retool and reorient production

- Stimulation of new industrial exports

- Housing privatization and the development of a rental market for housing, assisted by the World Bank to create private ownership and increase labor mobility

- Establishment of new, streamlined bankruptcy procedures to ensure the timely exit of loss-making enterprises

- Intensified conversion of the defense industry to new civilian production

- Rationalization of land use and other aspects of the agricultural system based on free market principles

- Rationalization of regional location of industries

With a move to income and value-added taxes, fiscal reform will be completed. This will include a complete reform of the mechanisms of household compensation. Household income will be taxed so as to make various kinds of social expenditure (such as for medical care, education, and housing) self-financing. As economic reform leads to an increase in unemployment, programs for retraining workers will be enacted and public-sector employment policies will be developed.

Official international financing will begin to decline during this period, as the Soviet Union's current account improves and private financial flows increase. In addition to the areas of industrial restructuring and housing, noted above, international support will take the following forms:

- Continuing but declining balance of payments support to enhance the macroeconomic stabilization program

- Structural adjustment loans of the World Bank to enhance the market efficiency in key sectors of the economy

- Support for investments in key infrastructure sectors

- Financial assistance for the emerging private sector through special private enterprise funds managed and led by the EBRD of joint investment projects

By the end of this period, in 1997, the private sector should be producing the major part of gross national product, and the integration of the Soviet economy into the world economy will be well advanced. As a result of the economic reforms, restructuring and investment, real incomes will have begun to grow, and living standards will be increasing.

Table 2
OVERTAKING THE CURRENT ECONOMIC CRISIS

CRISIS POINT	REMEDIAL MEASURES
1. Shortages of goods	• Liberalization of prices for basic goods • Import of goods by means including the balance of payments support fund, distribution of goods during initial period of price liberalization • Liberalization of economic activity and rapid restructuring of production favoring increased output of goods in demand
2. Fall in production	• Creation of competitive environment through liberalization of output volumes and prices, as well as removal of barriers to foreign trade • Privatization of state enterprises and revival of private incentives for economic activity • Commercialization of activity of government enterprises, and privatization of most of them • Stimulation of small and medium-size businesses • Increased availability of key foreign inputs, as a result of foreign exchange inflow • Restructuring of manufacturing, with increased production of consumer goods and reduced output of heavy industrial and military products • Implementation of investment programs, including use of foreign capital • Equalization of tax burdens on different industries
3. Inflation	• Elimination of "monetary overhang" through sales of government securities, primary jump in prices, devaluation of the ruble exchange rate, income from privatization • Stringent monetary and budget policy • Maintenance of stable exchange rate, using the currency stabilization fund

Table 2 *(continued)*

CRISIS POINT   REMEDIAL MEASURES

- Controls over wage levels
- Injections of goods during period of price liberalization, including use of imported goods

4. Unemployment
- Formation of unemployment benefit funds and state employment agencies
- Stimulation of private economic activity, in particular with development of small and medium-size businesses
- Organization of social work projects
- Export of labor (the new law on foreign travel takes effect)
- Stimulation of economic growth

5. Balance of payments deficit
- Introduction of current account convertibility of the ruble at a realistic exchange rate and stabilization of the exchange rate
- Exchange rate serves to encourage exports and provides market-based protection for domestic producers
- Achievement of payments balance with the assistance of financial inflows from the international financial institutions and industrialized nations
- Stimulation of foreign investment
- Export promotion through market analysis and development

6. Government budget deficit
- Coordination of USSR, republic, and local budgets upon conclusion of the Economic Union Agreement
- Reduction of government expenditure, particularly subsidies, defense spending and aid to foreign governments
- Tax reform
- Strict enforcement of government spending limits
- Implementation of new social programs only within the limits of the balanced budget

Table 3
MANAGEMENT OF THE ECONOMY UNDER COMMAND AND MARKET SYSTEM

COMMAND SYSTEM	MARKET SYSTEM
1. Mandatory state orders	• Sharp reduction in volume of orders following a switch to purchaser-seller relations between producer and consumer without government intervention • Government purchases to be based on market prices • Retention for the early months of 1992 of state orders with administrative price regulation in the defense sector (financed from the union budget), the pharmaceutical industry, and a very small number of other sectors • Retention for the first months of 1992 (until the formation of food markets) of an agricultural tax in kind (not to exceed 15 percent of output)
2. Administrative strengthening of existing economic ties	• Creation of a competitive environment with freedom to change business partners • Introduction of legislation on bankruptcy, legal liability for breach of contract, commercialization of state enterprises • Elimination of internal (interrepublic, interregional) barriers to the movement of goods • Sharp reduction of barter and related practices (e.g., "reciprocal supplies") as a result of the liberalization of prices and creation of an exchangeable currency

Table 3 *(continued)*

COMMAND SYSTEM	MARKET SYSTEM
3. Administrative price regulation	• Elimination of administrative control of prices, apart from a small number of exceptions previously agreed upon • Shift from administrative determination of prices to setting of prices through supply and demand (including imports), as in market economies • The government controls the overall level of prices *indirectly* through stringent monetary and budgetary policies • In addition the government affects the prices and available supplies of certain key commodities (food and medicines) during the price liberalization period *directly,* through distribution of goods from existing stocks (including Western supplies) • The government ensures the availability of basic amounts of essential foods through food coupons
4. Existence of multiple exchange rates and stringent currency controls	• Elimination of multiple exchange rates and transition to a single rate based on a devalued ruble • Introduction of convertible ruble for current account (exports and imports) • Support for the stabilization of the ruble based on stringent financial policies, the Currency Stabilization Fund, and Western support of the Soviet balance of payments • Ban on the use of foreign currency for internal payments • Substantial change of the system of hard currency payments to the government, normalizing the taxation of exchange earnings

Table 3 *(continued)*

COMMAND SYSTEM	MARKET SYSTEM
5. Administrative regulation of foreign trade	• Abolition of import and export licenses and quotas for almost all goods • Sharp reduction and standardization of import tariffs • Elimination of almost all export taxes, except energy, on which export taxes are to be phased out over three years • International competition stimulates the development of competitive domestic markets
6. Administrative regulation of credit to enterprises	• Restoration of a single national currency based on a newly created national central bank • Legislative limits imposed on the creation of money by the central bank • Indirect regulation of the financial system by the central bank • Establishment of reserve requirement for commercial banks • Establishment of a discount mechanism • Open market operations in government securities • Determination of interest rates by competitive commercial banks • Equity funds provided for the private sector in part through enterprise funds supported by international organizations • Elimination of the practice of writing off credits to enterprises

5

A PROGRAM FOR
WESTERN COOPERATION
AND ASSISTANCE

OVERVIEW OF SUPPORT NEEDED FOR
SOVIET ECONOMIC REFORMS

The magnitude and difficulty of the economic reforms that the Soviet Union must implement are unprecedented. Their consequences for the Soviet Union and for the rest of the world are potentially large.

The accelerating collapse of the Soviet economy makes the need for reform as well as aid both urgent and critical. Prices are rising rapidly and output is falling (by close to 10 percent in the first quarter of 1991). Foreign trade has plummeted (with imports estimated to have fallen by more than 40 percent in the first quarter of 1991).

Radical economic reorganization in a situation like

that of the Soviet Union, where output is already declining very rapidly, would produce massive economic dislocation, a collapse of investment and output, and dramatic declines in consumption. Under these conditions, the reform program would probably not be politically sustainable, and economic and political disintegration and chaos would be likely to follow.

In brief, the basic case for Western aid is that it would make democratization and transformation to a market economy possible by reducing the risk of economic and political chaos during a historically unprecedented reorganization of the economy and society. The financial resources provided by the West would prevent massive declines in the levels of consumption and investment in the Soviet economy during the transition—though it is anticipated that even with large-scale financial aid, output and consumption will decline during the early part of the transformation program. In addition, technical assistance, financial assistance, and international investments and joint ventures will restructure the Soviet economy, speeding the transition to a market economy and the return of economic growth.

A comprehensive Western aid strategy would be based on the following guidelines:

- Western economic aid will be conditional on the adoption and implementation of the economic reform program and on the continuation of the democratic reforms adopted in the Soviet Union. Conditionality will apply at each step of the process so that aid reinforces the momentum of reform. This means that the West will provide large-scale assistance if the Soviet leadership pursues a mutually agreed-upon reform program; if it does not, or if reform falters, then aid will not be disbursed.

- Western aid will be provided by a consortium of nations and international financial institutions. No single country will carry a disproportionate share of the financial burden of assistance. Participants in the program would most likely include the advanced industrial democracies, some other countries, the IMF, the World Bank, and the EBRD.

- Actual aid decisions will be made on the basis of discussions between and among the Soviet government, the Western governments providing aid, and international financial institutions. They will be based on a detailed assessment of the needs of the reform program and the capacity of the suppliers of aid.

- The aid program should be large. The judgment on the amounts should be based on an extension of calculations presented in the joint report on *The Economy of the USSR* produced by the IMF, the World Bank, the OECD, and the EBRD in December 1990, as well as ongoing discussions among the governments. The amount should reflect the political necessities of cushioning the decline in consumption and output that are likely to accompany the start of a tough reform program.

- Governmental contributions should come substantially in the form of grants rather than loans. As was true with the Marshall Plan, this will allow the Soviet Union to emerge from the transformation period without a debilitating debt burden. However, a part of the support from Western countries may come in the form of loans, which would imply a correspondingly lower economic burden for the donor governments and their citizens. Furthermore, support from international institutions will necessarily be in the form of loans.

The role and nature of aid should change during the course of the reform process. At the start, financial and commodity aid will be used primarily to finance the imports needed to prevent politically intolerable declines in consumption and output, and to sustain currency convertibility. As the reform process proceeds, aid will be used increasingly to finance investment in infrastructure and by the private sector through enterprise funds. For the initial three year period, foreign financial inflows will consist predominantly of official grants and loans; as the reform process takes hold, both the volume and share of official inflows will decline, as the current account of the Soviet Union improves and as private investment from abroad plays an increasingly important part.

Actual aid decisions will be made on the basis of discussions among the Soviet government, the bilateral aid providers, and the international financial agencies. They will be based on a detailed assessment of the needs of the reform program and the capacity of the suppliers of aid. We cannot at present undertake such an assessment, but can draw initially on the joint report on *The Economy of the USSR*. On the assumption that a reform program would not be put in place in 1991, at an oil price of $20, and with other assumptions that have turned out to be very optimistic, the joint report projected a financing requirement in hard currency of $27 billion; it identified financing of nearly

$17 billion, leaving a hard currency financing gap of $10 billion. The collapse of Soviet exports, with oil exports in particular down by nearly 50 percent, has led to a collapse of imports and worsened the economic decline in the first half of 1991. It is thus safe to estimate, on the basis of financial-gap analysis, that the Soviet Union would need an amount in excess of this hard-currency financing gap to initiate and sustain a reform process in 1991 and in subsequent years. We must emphasize that the final determination of the aid package should also take into account the political needs of managing the economic and democratic transformation.

In light of the economic collapse of the Soviet Union, and the political and economic stakes, we believe it wise to mount a large program, with some additional assistance being provided as early as the third quarter of 1991. The description of the sources of aid that follows is illustrative, designed to indicate the efforts that will be needed from the members of the international community.

The Marshall Plan transferred total resources from the United States of nearly 5 percent of one year's GNP over a four-year period. Treating the OECD countries as the donors, this would amount to $1 trillion ($1 thousand billion) over four years, far in excess of any imaginable aid program to the Soviet Union today. Thus any imaginable aid program, however large, would represent a much smaller effort for the donors than the Marshall plan. The needs of the Soviet economy now are greater in many ways than those of the European economies after World War II, for those economies primarily lacked physical capital, including inventories, and still had in place the market structures and human capital needed to operate them. The Soviet economy lacks both much of the needed human capital and market institutions, and—despite the high rates of investment under central planning—the relevant types of physical capital. Also, the social, political, and economic dislocations likely to accompany the Soviet economic transformation are daunting compared with those that faced the governments at the end of World War II.

It should be noted that the Marshall Plan aid was given overwhelmingly in the form of outright grants, rather than loans. This enabled the recipient countries to emerge from the reconstruction period without a debilitating debt burden. We recommend that the governmental contributions to the Soviet reform similarly come substantially in the form of grants (the support from the international institutions will necessarily be in the form of loans). We acknowledge, however, that a part of the support may come in the form of loans, which would imply a correspondingly lower economic burden for the donor governments and their citizens. This would also probably mean that the transfers to the Soviet Union in grants would be lower per capita than those given to Marshall Plan recipients.

The interests at risk when the Marshall Plan was introduced were immense. The success of the Marshall Plan and the recreation of a vibrant and prosperous Europe to which it led have brought us to the current situation, where the Soviet Union stands poised to join the democratic world. The stakes, and the potential rewards for generosity and imaginative statesmanship, are again enormous.

SOURCES OF FINANCIAL ASSISTANCE

The arrangements we describe below are typical of those that have succeeded in other cases, with the exception that the new EBRD has not yet played a significant role. The arrangements suggested here are, as is much else in this document, indicative of the arrangements that will in the end be decided by the Soviet Union together with the official international community. We address them explicitly mainly because the USSR is not yet familiar with the operations of the international organizations.

The specifics of financial assistance will be elaborated, on the principles just outlined, in the course of detailed negotiations between the Soviet Union and the international community in the coming months and years. The financial package should not only describe the amounts of assistance to be provided, but also the conditions for disbursing that assistance, and the relationship of specific kinds of assistance to specific steps in the reform program. Presumably, the negotiations will determine the detailed financial assistance to be provided in support of the Soviet reform program for the remainder of 1991 and for 1992, and will also provide general guidelines for assistance during the period 1993 to 1995.

There are four main sources of financial assistance:

The first is the International Monetary Fund, which makes loans in support of a nation's balance of payments on condition that the recipient carries out effective measures of stabilization and liberalization. The second is the World Bank, which carries out several kinds of activities: loans for infrastructure investments; loans to support major policy changes by the recipient government; and financial support for various kinds of technical assistance. The third source is the new European Bank for Reconstruction and Development, which was established in 1991 to support the transition to market-based democratic societies in Eastern Europe and the Soviet Union. The EBRD, like the World Bank, has a broad mission: lending for infrastructure investment; support for the development of the private sector in the economies in transition; and a range of technical assistance activities. Under its charter, at least 60 percent of EBRD funds must be used to promote the development of the private sector.

Finally, there are the Western governments themselves. In each of the Eastern European countries, support from international institutions has been augmented by direct support from governments. Some of that governmental support has been on a bilateral basis, for example when an individual Western European country pledges export credits to one of the reforming countries in Eastern Europe. Other government-to-government support has been on a multilateral basis, for instance through the European Community.

Countries undertaking large-scale reform programs have generally found it difficult to coordinate with the many different potential sources of government-to-government aid. In the 1989 Paris Summit, the G-7 leaders assigned responsibility for multilateral government-to-government aid to Hungary and Poland to the leadership of the European Community. In our view, it will also be necessary to coordinate bilateral and multilateral assistance to the Soviet Union.

There will also be a complex set of interactions among the major international financial institutions—the IMF, World Bank, and EBRD. While these interactions in the case of the Soviet Union will have to be worked out in the coming months and years, we note that working arrangements among the international financial institutions have been successfully arrived at many times in recent decades.

- The IMF will have principal responsibilities for oversight, lending, and advising in the areas of macroeconomic stabilization, the liberalization of prices, and the establishment of ruble convertibility. Since these steps constitute the initial objectives of the transformation program, the program of large-scale financial assistance should not begin until agreement has been reached between the Soviet Union and the IMF on an IMF-lending program to support stabilization and liberalization. In a precise sense, the first tranche of balance-of-payments support should be triggered by an agreement on an IMF letter of intent, to be completed late in 1991 or early in 1992. The next milestone will be the actual start of an IMF standby program early in 1992. World Bank and EBRD lending will not start until the IMF program is underway, though technical assistance from these institutions should commence earlier.

- The World Bank is likely to have the lead in lending and advising in areas related to structural adjustment. Initially, the key tasks of structural adjustment will involve the completion of a legal code consistent with a market economy based on private ownership; the establishment of a trade regime that supports the integration of the Soviet Union with the rest of the world market economy; and the implementation of new labor market programs such as unemployment insurance and job retraining centers that will provide a vital social safety net for workers displaced by the economic transition. Several specific areas of policy change overseen by the World Bank, such as trade liberalization or the establishment of a social safety net, should become the basis for policy-based World Bank loans (known as Structural Adjustment Loans, SALs, and Sector Adjustment Loans, SECALs).

The specific character of the World Bank's involvement will change during the course of the economic transformation. Policy-based lending in the early years will give way increasingly to project lending, that is, to loans for specific infrastructure projects. With regard to project loans, the goal for the World Bank will be to support projects that should properly be carried out by the public sector (such as roads, ports, or environmental control projects) as opposed to projects that can profitably be undertaken by the domestic or foreign private sector. Note that even as the lending shifts to projects, there will no doubt be a continuing need for some policy-based loans through 1995, for example to support banking reform, the conversion of military industry to civilian industry, and the privatization of agriculture and industry.

- The new EBRD was created with two main tasks in mind: to support the development of the private sector in Eastern Europe and the Soviet Union, and to support infrastructure investments in the region. The EBRD role in the Soviet Union is likely to have several components and could also involve other institutions. First, it would seek to establish new financial intermediaries that would channel financial support to private enterprises in the Soviet Union. For example, the EBRD should set up "private enterprise funds" along the lines of the Enterprise Funds that have been set up by the U.S. government in Hungary and Poland. Such funds would support new private firms in the Soviet Union both by making loans and by taking a direct equity stake in enterprises. The enterprise funds would channel a portfolio of investment money that includes not only EBRD funds but also funds from private-sector investors in the West that would participate in the EBRD-led institutions.

Second, the EBRD along with the World Bank could take the lead in establishing important new financial institutions within the Soviet Union, such as pension funds, mutual funds, and stock exchanges, that will play a vital role in the privatization process. Third, the EBRD along with other institutions can provide technical assistance regarding the operation of these new financial institutions.

There will inevitably be some overlap in the assignments of the three main international financial institutions. For example, the IMF, World Bank, and the EBRD will all share in providing technical assistance—an area in which many other agencies, including the European Community, are already active. The IMF and the World Bank both have expertise in such areas as financial-sector and fiscal reform. Similarly, the World Bank and the EBRD will share fundamental responsibilities in monitoring, advising, and providing financing for the privatization process. In general terms, however, it is possible to distinguish the main lines of responsibility of the World Bank and the EBRD. The EBRD would take the lead in devising ways to support the nascent private sector in the Soviet Union directly, while the World Bank focus would be mainly on structural adjustment issues and infrastructure investment that individually support the development of the private sector. To the extent that the EBRD undertakes infrastructure lending, it should be directed to projects that are closely related to its task of promoting the private sector, such as the establishment of stock exchanges, and should where possible accompany private sector financing.

International financial institutions can be expected to provide around half, or slightly less, of the total official financial assistance that will flow to the Soviet Union, while the rest will come from governments. Both the experience in Eastern Europe and in other countries in deep crisis, and calculation of the financing that each institution could provide, strongly suggest that the funds from international financial institutions are likely to be insufficient to meet the needs of successful transformation. The governments of advanced industrialized nations should provide two main kinds of direct support throughout the process. Initially, the most important support will be for balance of payments, in order to facilitate a smooth and successful implementation of price liberalization and currency convertibility. In later years, the support should shift increasingly to financing for infrastructure investment projects. Some government funding may also be needed to support projects that are predominantly financed by the private sector, for example, the development of a European-wide energy supply system integrating the Soviet Union with the rest of Europe.

The IMF and World Bank have long-established procedures of conditionality, that is, linking the disbursement of funds to the implementation of specific economic reform measures. These procedures will naturally be applied in the usual manner at each step of the economic assistance program. In negotiating a loan with the International Monetary Fund, for example, the Soviet Union will work with the IMF to prepare a detailed document which will describe the specific policy plans of the Soviet Union in the main economic spheres. The document, known as a Letter of Intent, will also detail a precise timetable of specific policy actions, and will contain various numerical performance criteria that will be the basis for judging whether the Soviet Union is fulfilling the policy plans as described in the economic program. Disbursements of money from the IMF will be made on a quarterly basis, and on the condition that the performance criteria have been achieved. If they have not been achieved, then discussions between the IMF and the Soviet Union would be required to ascertain whether continued lending would be justified following a modification of policies and performance criteria. Similar procedures will apply to World Bank loans, and it is to be expected that the EBRD, too, will work out modes of conditionality for its lending.

TYPES OF ECONOMIC ASSISTANCE

Generally speaking, there are five overlapping major types of targeted aid. The first is balance of payments support, by which we mean the provision of financial assistance (grants or loans), or the provision of specific imported goods (such as food or medicine), in order that the Soviet Union can import a greater overall amount than would otherwise be possible. The second is funding to support a Currency Stabilization Fund, by which we mean the provision of foreign exchange to the central bank of the Soviet Union, to help the bank stabilize the market value of the ruble after the ruble is made convertible. Third are funds for infrastructure investment, to allow the union and republic governments to carry out public investment projects that will be urgently needed to help the transformation to a market economy. A fourth kind of assistance is for private-sector development, based on loans or grants by the public sector in the West to new private-sector firms in the Soviet Union (such aid will be needed early in the transformation process to help build up the Soviet private sector; later in the process foreign private capital can be expected to flow into the Soviet private sector on a large scale). Fifth is technical assistance, which involves several different activities: training of workers, managers, and government officials for operating in the new market environment; expert advice on policy design; management advising to specific industrial enterprises; preparation of written texts. Technical assistance is both cheaper and qualitatively different from other forms of aid. Moreover, it can be targeted to critical sectors like agriculture and distribution and can be managed on a decentralized basis in the republics or even cities.

This kind of multifaceted aid program is normal for the Eastern European countries undergoing radical reforms, as well as for many countries in other regions of the world that are working with the international community to undertake fundamental policy changes. The program of assistance that we envision for the Soviet

Union will therefore build directly on the experience of many other reforming countries, and on the standard roles and procedures of the international institutions in supporting countries in the course of radical economic reforms. The procedures of the international institutions are time-tested, and provide extensive safeguards to the international community that the money will be used effectively in support of reform.

POSSIBLE TIMETABLE OF ECONOMIC ASSISTANCE

The timetable of financing must link up closely with the timetable of reforms. Indeed, in each step of the process, the nature and sources of finance are tied to the implementation of specific reform measures. At all stages of the process, however, there is the continuing and important need for technical assistance, both in the form of training of key personnel in governments and industry, and in the form of policy advising by the international community.

Preparatory Stage: June–December 1991

Technical assistance can and should begin immediately, in order to speed the reform process, and it will need to continue during the several years of transformation. During the remainder of 1991, there will be the need to prepare a broad program of technical assistance, including training of Soviet citizens for the new tasks of implementing a market economy. While the international institutions will provide much technical assistance, as will other official agencies, it is clear that assistance must go beyond those institutions, to include the participation of Western management and engineering experts in many key sectors in the Soviet Union, as well as the practical training of many Soviet counterparts in programs in the West. These exchange and training programs should be targeted on a significant scale, to allow thousands of experts from the West to come to the Soviet Union in any year, and tens of thousands of Soviet experts to travel to the West. International management and industry experts should participate in the work of task forces involved in analyzing the condition of various sectors of the Soviet economy and prepare recommendations for the reorganization of these sectors, taking into account the issue of attracting foreign investment. But the surest supply of tens of thousands who will transfer practiced "know how" about business plans, finance, marketing, and so forth, are international businessmen whose companies make investments and joint ventures.

Macroeconomic Stabilization and Market Reform: 1992

The widespread liberalization of prices and the unification and convertibility of the exchange rate will be carried out at the beginning of 1992. The process will be supported not only by the government-to-government balance of payments support but also by balance-of-payments-support loans from the IMF and the World Bank. We envision a one-year IMF standby loan that would be negotiated at the end of 1991 and begin early in 1992, as well as a World Bank Structural Adjustment Loan (SAL) that would also begin in the first half of 1992. The magnitude of the IMF loan will of course depend on the size of the quota that is set for the Soviet Union at the time of membership. Based on the size of the Soviet economy, and the formulas used to establish quotas for new members, it is reasonable to suppose that the quota would be at least $5.5 billion (and could well be much larger with a new quota increase for the IMF), and that the standby loan would be on the order of 90 percent of the quota, or $5 billion. The initial World Bank SAL could be on the order of $2 billion, to be followed by further lending later in the year.

At the time of the unification of the exchange rate and the establishment of convertibility, the Western governments would also finance a Currency Stabilization Fund to support the value of the ruble, of the sort that was established for Poland at the start of 1990. The Fund would provide a significant stock of foreign exchange reserves that would be available to the Central Bank of the Soviet Union for sales to the public at the new official exchange rate. The purpose of the fund is to give confidence to the Soviet public that the new value of the ruble will be stable by demonstrating that hard-currency reserves exist to sell to the public at the new official exchange rate. The knowledge that the Central Bank has access to a large stock of reserves should help to forestall a speculative attack on the ruble in which enterprises and households in large numbers suddenly attempt to convert their rubles to hard currency, out of fear of a ruble depreciation.

Under ideal circumstances, the Currency Stabilization Fund would hardly be used by the Central Bank. Rather, the mere availability of the fund would engender sufficient public confidence in the stability of the ruble that there would be no large-scale speculation against the currency. The size of the Currency Stabilization Fund should be analyzed carefully in the upcoming negotiations. As in Poland, after the operation of the stabilization fund for one or two years, the money in the fund could be converted into a combination of grants and long-terms loans to the Soviet Union (depending on the precise terms on which the fund is established).

During 1992, the governments would provide further balance of payments support. The key distinction between this balance-of-payments support and the Currency Stabilization Fund is that the balance-of-payments support is actually designed to be used. That is, the balance-of-payments support would be made available to the Soviet government in the expectation that the funds will be used to support the import of goods. To put it differently, the balance of payments support will help to finance a trade deficit of the Soviet Union in the initial stages of the reform program, so that living standards do not fall precipitously and social tensions worsen significantly during this phase. Of course, the size of the balance of payments support would, as is standard practice, be carefully integrated into the various performance criteria of the IMF-monitored program.

Balance of payments support can be provided in a variety of ways, and to either or both the union and republic governments. Some aid can come in the form of in-kind grants, for instance of food and medicines. Other balance of payments support would take the form of grants or loans.

During 1992, the EBRD would get started in its central mission of supporting private sector development. In addition to providing technical assistance, the EBRD would establish private-enterprise funds and other kinds of financial intermediaries, and would help to solicit private sector projects worthy of financial support from these new institutions. It would be desirable, for economic and political reasons, that the private enterprise funds should be established in each of the republics in the Economic Union. This will give an important sense to the people of the Soviet Union that the private sector development is not limited to major urban areas or to particular republics.

The overall amounts of aid in 1992 will only be determined in the course of future discussions and analysis, but we should stress that the sums needed to support a decisive reform program will be large, particularly in the first year of a program, when a social crisis could threaten the entire reform process. The initial adjustments in 1992 are both momentous and very difficult from the economic and political perspective. There is an urgent need to do all that is possible to establish a high level of confidence in the public and to limit the inevitable economic dislocations during the early periods of the reform, and thereby to help maintain the political and social viability of the program.

Strengthening of Stabilization, Large-Scale Privatization, and Structural Reform: 1993–1995

During 1993 to 1995, the overall international assistance program could usefully be put in the context of an Extended Fund Facility (EFF) negotiated with the IMF. An EFF is a three-year lending program based on a detailed program of policy actions defined over the course of the program. The program agreed to with the IMF runs in parallel with a three-year policy program agreed to at the same time with the World Bank. The amounts of IMF funding under the EFF should be similar to the flows under the standby arrangement.

During the 1993 to 1995 period, the World Bank would be expected to support the economic reform program in three ways. First, it could continue to provide balance-of-payments support in the form of Structural Adjustment and Sectoral Adjustment Loans. These policy-based loans will be vitally needed in several areas, including: the rehabilitation of the banking system along market lines; the commercialization and privatization of the agricultural sector; the conversion of military industry to civilian use; and other kinds of industrial restructuring to enable enterprises to survive and flourish in the new market environment.

Second, during this period the World Bank can be expected to increase its project lending. Urgently needed projects would include projects for environmental reclamation, transportation infrastructure, telecommunications, and military conversion. In all cases, the infrastructure loans should be carefully monitored to ensure that they do not compete with potential private-sector investments. Third, the World Bank is likely to provide important technical assistance throughout the period, in the form of training as well as policy advice.

The precise amounts of World Bank lending will of course be determined only in the course of future negotiations. We should stress, however, that the support should be significant, as befits a radical transformation program. It will be necessary for the overall flows to be consistent with World Bank practices on limiting the allocation of World Bank capital to any individual country to no more than 10 percent of the total of World Bank lending.

During the 1993 to 1995 period, the EBRD should accelerate its mobilization of support for the emerging Soviet private sector. The enterprise funds should begin operation, and, if they succeed, they should be able to transfer several billion dollars per year in funds from the private sector in the West to new Soviet private enterprises. In general, the EBRD's funds will be leveraged, and perhaps increasingly leveraged over time, in that each dollar channelled through EBRD-monitored financial institutions will represent a mix of EBRD money and private-sector capital from Western investors. Thus, the EBRD could transfer loans and equity capital to the new Soviet private sector at an increasing rate, as the private sector in the Soviet Union develops and as Western private funding grows.

The EBRD and other agencies' activities would continue in the design and implementation of new Soviet financial institutions geared toward rapid privatization of large industrial enterprises. During the 1993 to 1995 period, private mutual funds and pensions funds should begin to operate as significant institutions in the emerging private capital market in the Soviet Union. Of course, the international agencies and cooperating governments will be actively involved not only in the design of the institutions, and in attracting Western firms to help in their establishment and operation, but also in the practical and intensive training of Soviet personnel in the operation of these institutions.

As with the World Bank and the EBRD, Western governments will increasingly shift their aid during the 1993 to 1995 period away from straight balance-of-payments support and toward projects in infrastructure investment and the private sector. It is almost surely the case that balance of payments support will be needed in 1993 and 1994 to help sustain the flow of imports into the country, and thereby to help maintain social peace and the viability of the reform program through the difficult transformation period. At the same time, however, the governments can begin to think about supporting large-scale industrial development projects geared toward integrating the Soviet economy with the West. Overall flows from the governments can begin to decline during this period (dependent, of course, on the precise amounts being lent by the international institutions).

Significant private sector capital inflows should begin during this period, with the energy sector as a leading candidate. There are already detailed proposals for a European energy network and plan linking the Soviet Union and Western Europe. This concept is promising, though it needs much more extensive elaboration. It may require inflows of official funds in support of significant private-sector inflows. Market economies in Asia, similarly, might participate with the Soviet Union in the development of the vast resources in Siberia, primarily through their private sectors.

The overall sums needed for successful transformation during 1993 to 1995 are of course even more difficult to determine than the corresponding sums for 1991 and 1992. Again, we would like to stress that the transformation program is unlikely to be successful without extensive financial engagement by the West through 1995. However, the support needed from governments and the international institutions should decline markedly by the completion of the three-year EFF program in 1995. Starting in 1996, the bulk of the international capital flows to the Soviet Union should be in the form of private investment funds that are attracted by the new and growing market economy.

WHAT ABOUT THE MONEY?

The main subject of this report is not money. Our focus is the *transformation* of the Soviet Union to democracy and a market economy, and its *integration* into the world community. In the chapter on Soviet political and economic reform, we presented the Soviet program of economic and political transformation, and our common analysis of actions the West could take to maximize the probability of success. The program outlines steps that should be taken by Soviet leaders to advance the interests of the Soviet Union—whatever the West may do. But it is clear that Western actions will critically affect the probability of Soviet success.

If our basic argument is accepted, primary responsibility for the next stage lies with the Western governments and international financial institutions, in cooperation with the Soviet government. They must conduct the appropriate analyses and make their best professional judgment about the types of assistance to be provided, including money.

The amount of external assistance required depends first of all upon the Soviet Union's mobilization and use of its own resources: gold, oil, reductions in military expenditures, productivity improvements in its own industries, opening of investment opportunities, and other things. But if the West is prepared to repeat Marshall's pledge—"to assist so far as it may be practical for us to do so"—it must engage the Soviet Union in a process to answer what this means in detail.

If the leaders of the Soviet Union and the West can find a better concept of their relationship in the next phase than the strategic engagement proposed here, they will do so. But that concept will also require mutual commitments, some of which will cost money. The authors of this report believe that the defining question about the relationship proposed here should not be "how much does it cost?" Rather, leaders of the West and the Soviet Union should ask: "How much will it be worth?" When measured in terms of the value of success in this endeavor, the costs will be low—much less than costs imposed by the likely alternatives, and if provided sooner, lower than later.

6
WHAT IS TO BE DONE?

This paper is neither an exhaustive nor a definitive treatment of this extraordinarily important and complex subject. We lack the expertise and data necessary to give conclusive or specific advice about issues like the exact magnitude and form of Western assistance to the Soviet reform process. Rather, this study seeks to highlight for governments the urgency of problems relating to the future of the Soviet Union and its republics, and the Western industrial democracies' stakes in that future. Only interested governments, including the G-7 and the international financial institutions, have the resources and information to give this matter the sustained analytical attention it deserves. Only they can engage in the lengthy negotiation with Soviet au-

thorities to establish the pace, character, and details of
Soviet economic reform and Western financial and
technical support. And only Soviet and Western leaders can make the necessary decision to initiate this
process of mutual interaction.

APPENDIX

It has been suggested that our Joint Working Group should pursue several specific topics treated summarily in one or two paragraphs in this report. Members of the Working Group, and others with whom we have consulted in the preparation of this document, are preparing memoranda of 10 to 20 pages outlining concepts, principles and illustrative initiatives. Topics include:

- Food and distribution

- Defense conversion

- A Basic Framework for international investment

- A framework of natural resources investment

- Agricultural reform
- Trucking

We will be prepared to present these materials to the relevant governments if they are interested.